Modern Critical Interpretations
T. S. Eliot's
Murder in the Cathedral

Modern Critical Interpretations

These and other titles in preparation

Modern Critical Interpretations

T. S. Eliot's

Murder in the Cathedral

Edited and with an introduction by
Harold Bloom
Sterling Professor of the Humanities
Yale University

Chelsea House Publishers ◊ *1988*
NEW YORK ◊ NEW HAVEN ◊ PHILADELPHIA

Library of Congress Cataloging-in-Publication Data
T.S. Eliot's Murder in the cathedral / edited and with an introduction
   by Harold Bloom.
       p. cm.—(Modern critical interpretations)
    Bibliography: p.
    Includes index.
    Contents: The theological scene / Francis Fergusson — The
language of drama / Helen Gardner — The saint as tragic hero:
Saint Joan and Murder in the cathedral / Louis L. Martz — The new
rhythm / Carol H. Smith — Eliot and the living theatre / Katharine
Worth — Fear in the way / Michael Goldman — The pain of
purgatory / David Ward — Poetic drama / Stephen Spender — The
countersacramental play of signs / Michael T. Beehler — A liturgy
less divine / Robert W. Ayers — Murder in the cathedral and the
saint's play tradition / Clifford Davidson.
    ISBN 1–55546–037–2 (alk. paper)
    1. Eliot, T. S. (Thomas Stearns), 1888–1965. Murder in the
cathedral. 2. Thomas, à Becket, Saint, 1118?–1170, in fiction,
drama, poetry, etc. [1. Eliot, T. S. (Thomas Stearns), 1888–1965.
Murder in the cathedral. 2. English literature—History and
criticism.] I. Bloom, Harold. II. Series.
PS3509.L43M9 1988   87–27464
822'.912—dc19   CIP
                                                            AC

Contents

Editor's Note

This book brings together a representative selection of the best critical interpretations of T. S. Eliot's drama *Murder in the Cathedral*. The critical essays here are reprinted in the chronological order of their original publication. I am grateful to Hillary Kelleher for her assistance in editing this volume.

My introduction expresses some polite reservations as to Eliot's success in having found dramatic embodiment for his spiritual intentions. Francis Fergusson begins the chronological sequence of criticism with his analysis of "the action-suffering, knowing-unknowing formula" of the play, after which the late Dame Helen Gardner wonders if "a more simple and conventional treatment" of Thomas would have been worthier of "the truth and grandeur of the choruses."

The eminent scholar of the mode of religiomeditative poetry, Louis L. Martz, compares two saints as tragic heroes, Eliot's Saint Thomas and Shaw's rather less orthodox Saint Joan. In a defense of Eliot's play, Carol H. Smith argues that its effectiveness is the result of "the new and less lateral conception of rhythm which Eliot used."

Katharine Worth finds theatrical originality in the play, while Michael Goldman traces in *Murder in the Cathedral*'s design Eliot's central subject, self-loss and self-imprisonment. In David Ward's discussion, the emphasis is upon the drama's knowledge of the pain of Purgatory rather than its joy.

The poet Stephen Spender compares the play to Wagnerian opera, while Michael T. Beehler deconstructs *Murder in the Cathedral* as a "countersacramental" interplay of signs. In the reading of Robert W. Ayers, the drama is a liturgical act bordering upon the mode of apocalypse. Clifford Davidson concludes this volume by relating Eliot's work to the medieval tradition of saints' plays, and judging *Murder in the Cathedral* to have brought that past mode to life again.

Introduction

T. S. Eliot, for whom the *Essays* of Emerson were "already an encumbrance," to cite his own testimony, was haunted by transcendence, very much in the mode of his Emersonian ancestors, rather than in the more severe and traditional mode, Anglo-Catholic and Counter-Reformation, towards which he aspired. Michael Goldman argues that the fear of being haunted by transcendence is the central design of Eliot's dramas, including *Murder in the Cathedral.* Since *Murder in the Cathedral* was composed for the Canterbury Festival of June 1935, the play assumes that its audience will be at least ostensibly Christian. Francis Fergusson aptly applied to Eliot's Canterbury drama Pascal's analysis of the three discontinuous orders, nature, mind, charity, which Eliot had commended to "the modern world" in his introduction to the *Pensées.* On this reading, the Chorus are in the order of nature; Tempters, Knights and Priests belong to the order of mind; Thomas alone is in the transcendent order of charity.

Representing the order of divine love is, as all would agree, a rather difficult task, particularly upon a stage. Dante is the inevitable master here but no one would think of mounting a production of the *Paradiso. Sweeney Agonistes,* in my humble judgment, is by far Eliot's finest dramatic work, easily surpassing *Murder in the Cathedral* and its successors. Dame Helen Gardner, who admired both Eliot's poetry and his dogmatic convictions, admitted that the Canterbury drama lacked action and had an unconvincing hero, but found it "intensely moving and at times exciting when performed." I have attended only one presentation of the play, somewhat reluctantly, but my reactions are to be distrusted, even by me, since I am not precisely the audience Eliot had in mind. Eliot remarked, in his "Thoughts after Lambeth," that there could be no such thing as "a civilized non-Christian mentality." I wonder always at a view of civilization and its discomforts that

1

excludes Freud as the representative instance of a civilized mentality in our era, but then Eliot's literary survival does not depend upon his ideological tractates.

How authentic a literary achievement is *Murder in the Cathedral*? Both Francis Fergusson and Stephen Spender have compared it to Wagner's operatic texts, and Eliot, who shared little else with Bernard Shaw, was as Wagnerian as Shaw. In some sense, *Murder in the Cathedral* mixes Wagner and Shaw, creating an amalgam of *Parsifal* and *Saint Joan,* unlikely composite. Since Baudelaire, Milton, and Sophocles are echoed also, sometimes gratuitously, one sometimes wonders why Eliot ransacks the tradition as he does in *Murder in the Cathedral.* He may have felt that he needed all the help he could get, since his multiple allusions give the effect of baroque elaboration, rather than that of fulfilling or transcending dramatic and literary tradition.

If Eliot's purpose had been essentially liturgical, then the triumph of *Murder in the Cathedral* would be unquestioned, since the drama, as doctrine, would have constituted a preaching to the supposedly converted. A saint's play is a hard matter in our time, and Shaw managed it, barely, by joining his Joan to the mode of Bunyan. Eliot commends *Everyman* as the unique play within the limits of art, but *Murder in the Cathedral* hardly sustains comparison to *Everyman.* Well, an admirer of Eliot might reply, *Saint Joan* is not exactly of the eminence of *The Pilgrim's Progress,* but then Bunyan's great narrative is not a stage drama. How well does Eliot do in the dramatic representation of Archbishop Thomas Becket? All that I ever can remember of what Eliot's Becket says is the first part of his climactic speech, after the Chorus implores him to save himself so that they too can survive, and just before he preaches his Christmas Morning sermon, which ends part 1 of the play. The Women of Canterbury fear the coming change, whether it be transcendence or the withdrawal of transcendence. Thomas ignores them, since he is interested only in the final Tempter, who offers what he desires, and appears to be his true self. Does he reject that true self, or Fourth Tempter?

> Now is my way clear, now is the meaning plain:
> Temptation shall not come in this kind again.
> The last temptation is the greatest treason:
> To do the right deed for the wrong reason.
> The natural vigour in the venial sin
> Is the way in which our lives begin.

> Thirty years ago, I searched all the ways
> That lead to pleasure, advancement and praise.
> Delight in sense, in learning and in thought,
> Music and philosophy, curiosity,
> The purple bullfinch in the lilac tree,
> The tilt-yard skill, the strategy of chess,
> Love in the garden, singing to the instrument,
> Were all things equally desirable.
> Ambition comes when early force is spent
> And when we find no longer all things possible.
> Ambition comes behind and unobservable.

But how can you represent, dramatically, a potential saint's refusal to yield to his own lust for martyrdom? Eliot did not know how to solve that dilemma, and evaded it, with some skill. There is epigrammatic force in Thomas's crucial couplet, but is there dramatic insight as well?

> The last temptation is the greatest treason;
> To do the right deed for the wrong reason.

Let us, wickedly, experiment with altering that neat couplet:

> The last temptation is the greatest treason:
> To write a Christian play for the wrong reason.

It is no accident that Thomas's speech takes its pathos from Eliot's literary and intellectual career, the movement from searching all the ways available to an authentic contemporary poetry, on to the spiritual ambition that came when early force was spent. It is also no accident that the imagery of the Chorus of the Women of Canterbury grows increasingly violent, until the poor ladies seem to have become victims of their own pathological fantasies:

> I have smelt them, the death-bringers; now is too late
> For action, too soon for contrition.
> Nothing is possible but the shamed swoon
> Of those consenting to the last humiliation.
> I have consented, Lord Archbishop, have consented.
> Am torn away, subdued, violated,
> United to the spiritual flesh of nature,
> Mastered by the animal powers of spirit,
> Dominated by the lust of self-demolition,
> By the final utter uttermost death of spirit,

> By the final ecstasy of waste and shame,
> O Lord Archbishop, O Thomas Archbishop, forgive us,
> > forgive us, pray for us that we may pray for you, out
> > of our shame.

There is an oxymoronic rapture in that chorus that amounts to having the right rape performed upon one for the wrong reason. Thomas replies by assuring the women that: "This is one moment, / But know that another / Shall pierce you with a sudden painful joy." Presumably he prophesies his own martyrdom, which they are bound to misapprehend. His rather odd attempt at consoling them ends with one of the most famous of Eliotic lines: "Human kind cannot bear very much reality." Freud says much the same, but by "reality" he meant the authentic consciousness of one's own mortality. Eliot meant the breaking in upon us of the order of charity. Between the Chorus of the Women of Canterbury and the sanctified Thomas, every reader and playgoer chooses the Chorus, who save Eliot's drama from having to bear too much of a transcendent reality that evades dramatic representation.

*M*urder in the Cathedral:
The Theological Scene

Francis Fergusson

> *You know and do not know, what it is to act or suffer.*
> *You know and do not know, that acting is suffering,*
> *And suffering action. Neither does the actor suffer*
> *Nor the patient act. But both are fixed*
> *In an eternal action, an eternal patience*
> *To which all must consent that it may be willed*
> *And which all must suffer that they may will it,*
> *That the pattern may subsist, that the wheel may turn and still*
> *Be forever still.*
>
> Thomas to the Women of Canterbury, and the
> Fourth Tempter to Thomas

Murder in the Cathedral, considered simply as a modern play, owes a great deal to continental theater-poetry, which I have sampled in the work of Pirandello, Cocteau, and Obey. It is most closely akin, in its dramaturgy and its formal sense, to *The Infernal Machine:* it has a similar coherence for the eye of the mind, a comparable esthetic intelligibility. It may be regarded as a work of art in the same way. But it is based upon a different idea of the theater; it seeks a different (and far more radical) basis in reality. It was written for the Canterbury Festival, June 1935, and it takes the audience as officially Christian. On this basis the play is a demonstration and expression of the "right reason" for martyrdom and, behind that, of the right doctrine of human life in general—orthodoxy. It is thus theology, a work of the intellect, as the continental plays are not. *The Infernal Machine* and *Noah* represent

From *The Idea of a Theater: A Study of Ten Plays—The Art of Drama in Changing Perspective.* © 1949 by Princeton University Press.

5

myths; *Murder in the Cathedral* represents (by way of the story of Thomas à Becket) a type of *the* myth, the central, the basic myth of the whole culture. Only after its performance at the Canterbury Festival did it enjoy an after-life in the commercial theater in London, in our Federal Theater, and in the limbo of the academic theaters all over the world.

The continental plays came out of the theater, and Cocteau's phrase *poetry of the theater* applies to them accurately; but *Murder in the Cathedral* (in spite of its theatrical dexterity) did not. In this play Eliot is not so much a poet of the theater as a poet and theologian who uses the stage for his own purposes; and though he seems to have benefited from the Paris theater, he has no connection with any theatrical arts actually practiced in English. The play has some of the abstractness of *Everyman,* which Eliot has called the one play in English "within the limitations of art"; but he does not seek to reawaken this sense of drama, in the manner of Cocteau, for example, who with his "gloire classique," seeks to echo the not-quite-lost Baroque theatricality. In its conception, its thought, its considered invention of a whole idea of the theater, *Murder* is unique in our time; and it is therefore more important to investigate what kind of thing it is (and is not) than to reach any judgment of its ultimate value as drama.

The basic plot structure appears to be derived from the ritual form of ancient tragedy. The first part corresponds to the agon. The chief characters are the Chorus of Women of Canterbury, three Priests, four Tempters, and Thomas. The issue—whether and how Thomas is to suffer martyrdom for the authority of the Church—is most explicitly set forth in the scenes between Thomas and the Tempters, while the Priests worry about the physical security of the Church, and the Women suffer their premonitions of violation, a more metaphysical horror. The First Tempter, a courtier, offers pleasure, "kissing-time below the stairs." The Second, a Royalist politician, offers secular power, "rule for the good of the better cause." The Third, a baron, offers the snobbish comfort of acceptance by the best people, the security of the homogeneous class or tribe. These three echo motivations from Thomas's past, which he has completely transcended, and can now dismiss as "a cheat and a disappointment." But the Fourth Tempter offers Thomas the same formula ("You know and do not know, what it is to act or suffer") which Thomas had himself offered the Women when he first appeared; and he shows Thomas that his acted-suffered progress toward martyrdom is motivated by pride and aims at "general grasp of spiritual power." For the first time, Thomas nearly despairs:

"Is there no way, in my soul's sickness / Does not lead to damnation in pride?" he asks. There follows a chorus in four parts, triumphant Tempters, Priests, and Women, envisaging and suffering Thomas's danger in their various ways; after which Thomas sees his way clear, the "right reason" for suffering martyrdom. This is the climax and peripety of Thomas's drama and the dramatic center of the play; and I shall consider it in more detail below. It concludes the first part.

There follows an Interlude: Thomas's Christmas sermon addressed directly to the audience. He sets forth the timeless theory of the paradox of martyrdom: mourning and rejoicing, living and dying in one: the bloody seed of the Church. From the point of view of the dramatic form, it corresponds to the epiphany following the agon and the choral pathos of part 1. It is also another demonstration, in another mode of discourse and another theatrical convention (the sermon), of the basic idea of the play.

Part 2 is, from the point of view of Thomas's drama, merely the overt result, the more extended pathos and epiphany, of his agon with the Tempters: he merely suffers (and the audience sees in more literal terms) what he had foreseen at the end of part 1. This part of the play is in broad, spectacular effects of various kinds. First there is the procession of the Priests with banners commemorating three saints' days: those of St. Stephen, St. John the Apostle, and the Holy Innocents. The four Knights (who replace the Tempters of part 1 and, as a group, correspond to them) come to demand that Thomas yield to the King, and then they kill and sanctify him at once. The killing is enacted in several steps, including a chorus in English (one of the best in the play) while the Dies Irae is sung offstage in Latin. After the killing the Knights advance to the front of the stage and rationalize the murder in the best British common sense political style. The immediate effect of the Knights is farcical—but, if one is following the successive illustrations of the idea of the play, their rationalization immediately fits as another instance of wrong reason. If it is farce, it is like the farce of the Porter in *Macbeth:* it embodies another aspect of the subject of the play. Part 2 as a whole, corresponding to a Shakespearean last act and to the catastrophe with chorus and visual effects at the end of a Greek tragedy, is rhythmic, visual, exciting, and musical—contrasting with part 1 which is addressed essentially to the understanding.

Though the form of the play is derived from ritual tragedy, it is far more abstractly understood than any traditional ritual tragedy. It is based not only upon Dionysian but also upon Christian ritual, and upon the resemblance between them. The human scene, or social focus, is generalized in the same way: the Cathedral is neither Canterbury in 1935 nor Canterbury in 1170 but a scheme referring to both, and also to a social order like that which Sophoclean tragedy reflects; a three-part order consisting of the people, individuals with responsible roles in church or state, and the shepherd of the flock who is responsible for the tribal religion. Hence the dramatis personae are, in their initial conception, not so much real individuals as roles in the life of the schematic community: there are resemblances between Knights and Tempters, and between both and the Priests, which deprive all of them of complete individuality and point to ideas which the stage figures represent. The peculiar qualities of the play—its great intellectual scope and distinction as well as its allegorical dramatic style—rest upon the abstractness of its basic conception, so unlike that of ritual drama in a living tradition. The best place to study the scheme, or the dramatic machinery of the play, is Thomas's peripety at the end of part 1.

The ways which Eliot finds to represent Thomas at the crucial moment of his career are entirely unlike those by which Obey presents his Noah. Obey makes-believe Noah as a real man and "God's world" as real. He then shows Noah living moment by moment, in the alternation of light and darkness, and in the palpable effort to obey his *Deus Absconditus:* he appeals to our direct perception and to analogies in our own experience. Eliot does not seek to grasp Thomas imaginatively as a person; he rather postulates such a man, and places him, not in God's world but in a theological scheme. He then indicates both the man and his real, i.e., theological, situation indirectly by means of the significant elements which he assembles: Tempters, Priests, and Chorus of Women.

The first three Tempters do not tempt Thomas, because he is completely beyond the temptations they offer. They set forth three forms of temptation which are not so much realized in human character as expressed in the varied music and imagery of their verse. The Fourth Tempter does not really tempt Thomas either: he reveals a temptation to which Thomas is in danger of succumbing; but as soon as Thomas sees it, it ceases to be a temptation and becomes the instrument of purgatorial suffering. From this suffering come Thomas's desperate questions or appeals, ending with "Can I neither act nor suffer / Without perdition?" To which the Fourth Tempter replies with the action-passion paradox which I have quoted. There follows a choral passage in four parts which, in its development, resembles what

Thomas must be undergoing. The four Tempters chant their triumph-ant despair: "Man's life is a cheat and a disappointment." The Priests utter their very secular fright: "Should we not wait for the sea to subside?" The Chorus, the Priests, and the Tempters in alternation present a vision of horror: "Death has a hundred hands and walks by a thousand ways." The Chorus then appeals to Thomas: "God gave us always some reason, some hope," they chant, "but now a new terror has soiled us"; and the passage concludes,

> O Thomas Archbishop, save us, save us, save yourself that
>   we may be saved;
> Destroy yourself and we are destroyed.

To which Thomas answers (though, it seems, not directly to the Chorus):

> Now is my way clear, now is the meaning plain:
> Temptation shall not come in this kind again.
> The last temptation is the greatest treason:
> To do the right deed for the wrong reason.

He then thinks over his career as he now sees it: his deluded pursuit of worldly triumphs, pleasures, and powers—talking to himself or the audience rather than to any of the figures onstage.

The difficulty of this passage is in grasping Thomas's peripety (or conversion) dramatically; and this is a matter both of the action Eliot is imitating and of the means he uses.

The chief means is the four-part chorus. *Murder* is the only mod-ern play in which the chorus is an essential part of the dramatic scheme, and here the chorus plays a role similar in several respects to that of the Sophoclean chorus: i.e., it expresses, in the music and imagery of verse, if not what Thomas suffers, at least the suffering (depraved or painful) which results from Thomas's peril—a suffering similar to his yet on a completely different level of awareness, as the suffering of the Sophoclean chorus, in its real but mysterious world, is not. This chor-us also reveals to Thomas the "right reason" (charity) for his martyr-dom; but here again it does so without understanding anything itself, whereas the Sophoclean chorus, dim though its awareness is, to some degree shares a sense of the final good of all. We must suppose that Thomas hears their chanted appeal, and sees thereby the will of God (as distinguished from his own ambitious or suicidal will) in his progress toward martyrdom. Thus Eliot has arranged the elements of his compo-sition in such a way that we may (like Thomas himself) deduce both his change of heart and his right reason at this point—but we may do so only in the light of the orthodox doctrine, the theological idea, of martyrdom.

But Eliot carefully does not show this change in Thomas himself at this point. If we attempt to imagine him as a real man in a real situation—as an actor would be impelled to do if he were trying to act the role—we may either say that he has found a new and better rationalization for the same deathly and power-mad impulse which drove him before, and thus achieved simply another intellectual feat, or else that the sudden intervention of Grace has removed him to a realm which is completely invisible to us. For Thomas himself remains invisible: he gives nothing, except the very interesting summary of his past and dead worldly career as the Tempters revealed it to him. Later—in the Christmas sermon—he will give his reasons at length and in very general terms; and after that, his life.

Before considering the allegorical dramaturgy and the peculiar theology underlying this passage, it should be pointed out that it cannot be understood apart from the whole play, which is all a demonstration and expression of Thomas and his sanctification. The sermon explains it, and part 2 of the play shows it in comparatively realistic terms. I have said that part 1 corresponds to the agon; and it does certainly complete Thomas's own drama: "I shall no longer act or suffer, to the sword's end," he says at the end of it. But if one thinks of the "drama" as the actual dispute with the drunken Knights, followed by the real killing, then part 1 may be considered a "Prolog im Himmel" which establishes the theological scene; and on this view its very abstract style is easy to justify. But the theological scene is presented as the sole reality; and in the realistic horrors of part 2 everything moves by its machinery—the drunken evil of the killers, the reflex fluttering of the Priests, the abandoned and Wagnerian somnambulism of the Chorus, and even Thomas, who goes through the motions without conviction, or rather with a conviction which is not literally represented at all:

> It is out of time that my decision is taken
> If you call that decision
> To which my whole being gives entire consent.
> I give my life
> To the Law of God above the Law of Man.
> Those who do not the same
> How should they know what I do?

as he puts it to the totally uncomprehending Priests. Realistic though part 2 is, in a way, its reality is at the same time denied; and it is composed according to the same formal principle, and in illustration of the same idea, as part 1.

The purpose, or final cause, of the play is the demonstration of a particular theological idea which one must attempt to grasp if the play is to be understood. Mr. Eliot wrote of Pascal, in his introduction to the *Pensées*: "Capital, for instance, is his analysis of the *three orders:* the order of nature, the order of mind, and the order of charity. These three are *discontinuous;* the higher is not implicit in the lower as in an evolutionary doctrine it would be. In this distinction Pascal offers much about which the modern world would do well to think." This notion throws a good deal of light upon the schematic scene of *Murder in the Cathedral.* The Chorus would be in the order of nature; the Tempters, Priests and Knights in the order of the mind; and Thomas in the order of charity. Only the first two orders are visible to us, unless by Grace; but it is only in the order of Charity that Thomas and the form and meaning of the whole are finally intelligible. In the play, this order is represented by the doctrine which Thomas expounds in the sermon, and also by the abstract scheme of the play: the "three orders" and the three parts of society. Hence the mechanical feel of the play as a whole: the dramatis personae are as discontinuous from each other and from any common world as the parts of a machine, but they move according to the will of God as that is represented by (and deducible from) the theological doctrine. It is an idea of the divine plan, and of human experience as subject to it, which comes out of modern idealism: one is reminded of Leibniz's preestablished harmony. Is this the way in which we must now understand Christianity? I do not know. And I do not assume that Mr. Eliot himself would say so. But it is the doctrine which this play demonstrates; and in the play, therefore, the whole realm of experience represented by the *Purgatorio,* the direct sense of moral change (not to be confused with evolution), of natural faith, and of analogies which make the three orders not completely discontinuous—in short, the whole appeal to a real world which all may in some sense perceive—is lacking.

On this basis one must understand the paradoxical notion of action which the play presents, and thence its dramatic form. The formal cause of the play (the clue to the plot, to the use of the stage, to the characterization, and to the verbal medium) is the idea of action expressed in the formula, "You know *and do not know* that acting is suffering / And suffering action."

In the play this formula works as a governing formal idea; but to avoid misunderstanding it is necessary to point out that this idea is itself poetic, and derived from experience—from that direct sense of human life which I have been calling histrionic. The histrionic basis of Eliot's verse has often been pointed out; it is the source of its unique and surprising vitality. He is a metaphysical poet by instinct; he imitates action by the music and imagery of his verse, or he defines it, or he does both at once:

> The child's hand, automatic
>
> . . . .
>
> My friend, blood shaking my heart,
> The awful daring of a moment's surrender
>
> . . . .
>
> The lost heart quickens and rejoices
> At the lost lilac and the lost sea voices.

The action-suffering formula may be regarded as an achievement, in the medium of metaphysical poetry, for which all of Eliot's work up to that time had been a preparation. But part of this preparation must have been the study of the great dramas of the tradition; and the best way to grasp the scope of the formula is to compare it with the notions of action in three landmarks which I have studied [elsewhere]: the tragic rhythm of Sophocles, the rational action of Racine, and the passionate action of Wagner.

The Sophoclean tragic rhythm spreads before us, in time, a spectrum of modes of action, from reasoned purpose, through suffering informed by faith, to a new perception of the human creature: the moment of the "epiphany." The whole movement occurs in time; and when, at the end of a figure, we see the human creature in a new light, it is still the human creature that we see, in a world continuous (by analogy) with that of common sense. It is only by means of this tragic rhythm repeated in varied figures that the action of the play as a whole is conveyed, also by analogy: and what is conveyed is not a verbal formulation but an action which we are invited to apprehend sympathetically and histrionically. Eliot's action-suffering formula is a generalization derived from the tragic rhythm; and it seeks to fix human action (beneath the "masquerades which time resumes") as it timelessly *is* in the hand of God. The tragic rhythm as such disappears when thus abstractly considered; and the elements of Eliot's composition are regarded not as imitations of the one action but as illustrations of the one eternal formula.

In this respect *Murder in the Cathedral* is closely akin to the "ideal" dramas of Racine and Wagner, which celebrate respectively action as rational, and action as passion (or suffering). The action–suffering paradox comprehends the complementariness of reasoned purpose and mindless passion which I endeavored to point out [elsewhere] when considering Racine and Wagner. But though the notion of action in *Murder* seeks to comprehend and transcend Racine's and Wagner's visions, it implies, like them, the univocal sense of form and the idealist principles of composition. Thus the ideal perfection of the chorus is due to the fact that it exists primarily (like *Tristan*) as the expression, in music and imagery, of a mode of suffering, and only secondarily as "The Women of Canterbury": the performers would make it come alive by understanding the music rather than by understanding poor old women. And so for the Priests, Tempters, and Knights: they are demonstrations, and expressions in imagery, of rationalizations first, and men second, as though by an afterthought. The dramatis personae (essences of discontinuous worlds of experience) have nothing in common but the blank and meaningless fact of the killing—except Thomas. He knows what he act-suffers as the rest do not. The "basis in reality," which Mr. Eliot says every convention must have, is in Thomas's invisible moment of illumination, "the occupation of a saint." Thus a unique relation between author, performers, and audience is established: they are as discontinuous (and "perfect") as the dramatis personae. The perfection of the choral music, the elegance of the reasoned demonstrations by Tempters, or Priests, or by Thomas in his sermon, is gained by accepting completely the limitations of a superidealist convention. Hence the nightmarish feel of the play: all is explicit and expressed, yet all moves by unseen machinery and speaks by ventriloquism. This sense of dramatic form is akin both to the "despotic ideal" which Baudelaire felt in Wagner's orchestration, and to the a priori and almost actor-proof perfection of the Racinian Alexandrines.

If one considers, not the perfection of the discontinuous parts of the play but the perfection of the whole, it appears that all the parts are instances of the action-suffering, knowing-unknowing formula. It is in this way that the play as a whole coheres in the eye of the mind: the general scheme has the beauty of the perfectly formed and aptly illustrated thought. In Mr. Eliot's three orders, the realm of the mind would appear to be in some sense higher than that of nature, where his

Chorus suffers in complete mindlessness. And he seems to have proposed to himself a dramaturgic problem like that which Corneille tackled in *Polyeucte,* and Cocteau in *The Infernal Machine:* to show, in the mirror of reason, a change of heart. He might have taken as his motto and principle of composition Cocteau's suggestive remark, "Resemblance is an objective force which resists all the subjective transformations. Do not confuse resemblance with analogy." Thus the form of the play is most closely akin to the masterpieces of the Rationalist tradition.

But Mr. Eliot parts company with this tradition, even more radically than Cocteau, by explicitly denying the reality of that "order of mind" in which the art of the play is legible:

> Those who do not the same,
> How should they know what I do?

asks Thomas. To this question there can be no reply. The play does not rest upon direct perception or natural faith; it does not base itself upon analogies in common experience. It does not assume that reason and the "mirror of reason" capture the truth of the human situation: it rests upon revealed truth, which can only reach us here below in the form of the paradoxical formulas of theology, at once reasoned and beyond reason. From the concepts of theology all is deduced: the very idea of a theater as well as the clue to the form of the play and the selection of illustrations. One might put it that the purpose, or final cause, of the play, which distinguishes it from any other drama, is precisely to demonstrate and express the priority, the sole reality, of this same final cause.

But, while recognizing the unique purpose of the play, I wish to study its formal rather than its final cause: to consider it as drama rather than theology. And I wish to offer two observations upon it as an example of the art of imitating action.

The first is that, whatever one may think of its theology and its epistemology, it cannot be dismissed as simply "unreal." It almost completely eschews photographic or modern realism; but the sense of human action which it conveys is very much like that which we get from other first-rate modern drama with a strong intellectual and ethical motivation, Ibsen's and Pirandello's for example. If one learns to understand the extremely consistent conventions of *Murder in the Cathedral,* one may read it as an imitation of that human action which we know from a thousand other sources: human life divided by the machinery of the mind, and confined by the greedy idolatries of the sensibility. The theological "basis in reality" which Eliot accepts may be regarded as an interpretation reached inductively through this common experience, even though Eliot presents it as the truth from which all is deduced.

The second observation follows from the first: in spite of its absolute finality and its ideal perfection, *Murder in the Cathedral* should be regarded as employing only one of many possible strategies for making modern poetic drama—which is as much as to say that the problem has not been solved in the sense of Sophoclean or Shakespearean drama. Mr. Eliot himself has explored other modes of action and awareness, other, less idealized relationships between poet and audience, both in his verse and in his other plays. I have quoted some of the explicit imitations of action to be found in his verse. In *The Rock,* the reality of time and place, of the historic moment, is explored as it is not in *Murder in the Cathedral.* In *Family Reunion* Mr. Eliot seems to be seeking a more realist type of dramaturgy; and he seeks it (like Obey in *Noah*) in the complex and prerational relationships of the Family. In short, Mr. Eliot's own practice in his other works invites us to consider *Murder in the Cathedral,* in spite of its perfectionism, not as the drama to end all dramas but as one example of the art in our confusing times.

Hence the purpose of placing it in relation to Cocteau's and Obey's poetries of the theater. As imitations of action, the three plays are comparable; three attempts to bring the light of the tradition to bear upon the contemporary human; three partial perspectives of great value and suggestiveness. A contemporary idea of the theater, if we had it, would leave room for them all as well as for some of the values of modern realism which modern poetry of the theater, or in the theater, has to do without.

The Language of Drama

Helen Gardner

> I gotta use words when I talk to you
> But if you understand or if you don't
> That's nothing to me and nothing to you.
> Sweeney in Sweeney Agonistes

> Those who do not do the same
> How should they know what I do?
> How should you know what I do? Yet how much more
> Should you know than these madmen beating on the door.
> Thomas in Murder in the Cathedral

> I can only speak
> And you cannot hear me. I can only speak
> So you may not think I conceal an explanation,
> And to tell you that I would have liked to explain.
> Harry in The Family Reunion

The martyrdom of Becket was an obvious choice for a Canterbury play, made more attractive no doubt by the association of the saint's name. The theme of the conflict of the spiritual and the secular powers, the relation of church and state, was topical, and is a subject on which Mr Eliot has spoken much in prose. The story of Becket's life would seem to hold great dramatic and tragic potentialities, for the "deed of horror" takes place between persons who, though not closely related, as Aristotle thought best, were at least closely bound by old ties of friendship; and the deed has a peculiar horror by the addition of sacrilege to the guilt of murder. But although the conflict of church and state is present in the play, it is subordinated to another theme, and the drama of personal relationships Mr Eliot deliberately avoids. The king

From *The Art of T. S. Eliot.* © 1950 by Cresset Press Ltd.

17

does not appear and the knights are not persons, but at first a gang, and then a set of attitudes. They murder for an idea, or for various ideas, and are not shown as individuals, disturbed by personal passions and personal motives. The central theme of the play is martyrdom, and martyrdom in its strict, ancient sense. For the word martyr means witness, and the church did not at first confine the word to those who sealed their witness with their blood; it was a later distinction that separated the martyrs from the confessors. We are not to think of a martyr as primarily one who suffers for a cause, or who gives up his life for truth, but as a witness to the awful reality of the supernatural. The actual deed by which Thomas is struck down is in a sense unimportant. It is not important as a dramatic climax towards which all that has happened leads. We are warned again and again that we are not watching a sequence of events that has the normal dramatic logic of motive, act, result, but an action which depends on the will of God and not on the wills of men:

> For a little time the hungry hawk
>> Will only soar and hover, circling lower,
>> Waiting excuse, pretence, opportunity.
>> End will be simple, sudden, God-given.

Nothing prepares us for the consummation. We are told rightly that

>> the substance of our first act
> Will be shadows, and the strife with shadows.

Thomas can hardly be said to be tempted, for the play opens so near its climax that any inner development is impossible. Except for the last, the temptations are hardly more than recapitulations of what has now ceased to tempt, an exposition of what has happened rather than a present trial; and the last temptation is so subtle and interior that no audience can judge whether it is truly overcome or not. "Solus Deus cogitationes cordium cognoscere potest." What spiritual pride lurks in a martyr's heart, even in his last agony, is not to be measured by the most subtle and scrupulous self-analyst, far less by any bystander. Though Thomas may say

> Now is my way clear, now is the meaning plain:
> Temptation shall not come in this kind again,

a question has been raised that cannot be answered dramatically and that has simply to be set aside. We have to take it for granted that

Thomas dies with a pure will, or else, more properly, ignore the whole problem of motives as beyond our competence and accept the fact of his death. If in the first act the strife is with shadows, in the second there is no strife at all. The martyr's sermon warns us that "a martyrdom is never the design of man," and that a Christian martyrdom is neither an accident nor "the effect of a man's will to become a Saint." The hero has only to wait for his murderers to appear:

> All my life they have been coming, these feet. All my life
> I have waited. Death will come only when I am worthy,
> And if I am worthy, there is no danger.
> I have therefore only to make perfect my will.

When the knights rush in the momentary drama of their irruption breaks against the calm of Thomas, and the murder takes place as a kind of ritual slaughter of an unresisting victim, a necessary act, not in itself exciting or significant.

The attempt to present in Thomas the martyr in will and deed, with mind and heart purified to be made the instrument of the divine purpose, is a bold one. Success is hardly to be expected. There is more than a trace in the Archbishop of the "classic prig" who disconcerts us so deeply in Milton's presentation of the tempted Christ in *Paradise Regained.* There is a taint of professionalism about his sanctity; the note of complacency is always creeping into his self-conscious presentation of himself. He holds, of course, the pastoral commission, and it is right that he should teach his flock, but his dramatic function comes to seem less to be a martyr or witness, than to improve the occasion, to give an Addisonian demonstration of "how a Christian can die." Thomas is indeed less a man than an embodied attitude, for there is in this play an almost Gnostic contempt for personality and its expression in acts. When Thomas declares with some scorn

> You argue by results, as this world does,
> To settle if an act be good or bad.
> You defer to the fact,

he seems to have forgotten that the test of fruits is not only the world's test; it is deeply in the Gospels. When he announces "I have only to make perfect my will," he speaks more as a Gnostic Sage than as a Christian Saint. Sanctity here appears too near to spiritual self-culture. The difficulty lies partly in the nature of dramatic presentation. The protagonist of any play must be conscious and aware; that is part of his function as protagonist. It is through him that the situation is made clear to us, and we recognize implications hidden from other persons in the drama. But if there is no true action, if the centre of the play is a state of mind, the protagonist can only be *self*-aware and self-conscious, and self-consciousness is incompatible with sanctity. Mr Eliot has conceived his hero as a superior person. The nature of his superiority can be expounded dramatically only by himself, for the play assumes a gulf between the saint and the ordinary man. Inevitably in the expounding the protagonist appears superior in the pejorative sense.

But for all its lack of action and its unconvincing protagonist, *Murder in the Cathedral* is intensely moving and at times exciting when performed. The real drama of the play is to be found in fact where its greatest poetry lies—in the choruses. The change which is the life of drama is there: from the terror of the supernatural expressed at the opening to the rapturous recognition of the "glory displayed in all the creatures of the earth" in the last. The fluctuations of the chorus are the true measure of Thomas's spiritual conquest. They feel his failure of faith after the last temptation. They know obscurely that if sanctity is nothing in the end but a higher egoism, there is no value in any human goodness. Only if the heroic has meaning can the ordinary have dignity. They "know and do not know"; for they feel the danger but mistake where safety lies:

> God is leaving us, God is leaving us, more pang, more pain,
> > than birth or death.
> Sweet and cloying through the dark air
> Falls the stifling sense of despair;
> The forms take shape in the dark air:
> Puss-purr of leopard, footfall of padding bear,
> Palm-pat of nodding ape, square hyaena waiting
> For laughter, laughter, laughter. The Lords of Hell are here.

If he is safe, they are safe too; if he is destroyed, they are destroyed. They implore him to save himself for their sake, but the safety he and they find is of another kind. They have to learn that there is no safety in flight, and no escape in obscurity from evil and death. They have to accept their share in the "eternal burden, the perpetual glory": the burden of sin, the glory of redemption. In the great chorus before the martyrdom they identify themselves with a whole world groaning and travailing. The monstrous act they are about to witness is not an aberration, an eccentricity; it is an expression of the universal malice and corruption, which it is man's burden and glory to be conscious of. It is not something of which the common man is innocent. The evil plotted by potentates is the same evil as is met

> in the kitchen, in the passage,
> In the mews in the barn in the byre in the market place
> In our veins our bowels our skulls.

They have to pierce deeper, beyond all agents and forms of evil, beyond death and judgment to

> Emptiness, absence, separation from God.

In face of the intensity of the Dies Irae chorus, the ecstasy of penitence and shame that breaks out with the cry

> Clear the air! clean the sky! wash the wind! take stone from
> stone and wash them,

and the final chorus of praise, criticism of the presentation of the hero seems irrelevant; it is only a minor blemish. Although we may not get from *Murder in the Cathedral* the experience we normally look for in a play, the experience we do get cannot be called anything but dramatic. We identify ourselves with the women of the chorus; their experience communicates itself to us, and gives us the feeling we have been not spectators but sharers in a mystery. We live through a *peripeteia,* we experience a great discovery. We pass with them through horror, out of boredom, into glory.

Once again Mr Eliot has in fact gone back in order to go forward. He has returned to the most primitive form of tragedy. The model is the earlier plays of Aeschylus in which, as Professor Murray says,

> There is one great situation, in which the poet steeps our minds, with at most one or two sudden flashes of action passing over it. Woman pursued by the lust of unloved man, the Saviour of mankind nailed eternally to the rock, the suspense of a great people expecting and receiving the news of defeat in war, the agony of a besieged city—these are all the kind of subject that might be treated in a simple choral dance with nothing but words and music. At most Aeschylus, transforming the *Molpê* into drama, adds a brief flash of action: in the *Supplices* the rescue of the women, in the *Prometheus* the binding in the prologue and the casting into Hell at the end, in the *Seven* the scene where Eteocles goes out to kill his

brother and to die. In the *Persae* there is a steady tension throughout, diversified by the entrance of the Messenger, the evocation of Darius, and the entry of Xerxes, but the situation is never changed, only seen from different angles.

When Professor Murray sums up Greek tragedy in a sentence, his words could be applied to *Murder in the Cathedral:* "Normally the play portrayed some traditional story which was treated as the *Aition* or origin of some existing religious practice." Mr Eliot, invited to write a play for Canterbury, has begun where the earliest Greek dramatists would have begun, with the present fact: the veneration paid to the martyr by the Church for which he died. His play leads to its last words: "Blessed Thomas pray for us." The poor women of the chorus are prototypes of all those who, throughout the ages, will come to implore help from the hero-saint. They are the worshippers at the shrine, the pilgrims to Canterbury, the Christian equivalent of the ritual mourners weeping for the dead god or hero. But the play transcends its origin and occasion, and the chorus becomes humanity, confronted by the mystery of iniquity and the mystery of holiness.

Murder in the Cathedral is like *Ash-Wednesday* in its choice of a Christian theme, its employment of liturgical material: the introits and versicles for the three days after Christmas, the Dies Irae, the Te Deum; and most of all in the contrast between the ideal of sanctity, which is at the centre, and the reality of the experience of common unsanctified humanity out of which both poem and play arise. But the symbolic figures of *Ash-Wednesday,* by whom the idea of blessedness is communicated—the Lady of Silences and the veiled sister, existing in a world of dream and vision—are more satisfying to the imagination than Thomas, who has to endure the hard, clear light of the stage. Perhaps Mr Eliot tried too much with Thomas, and a more simple and conventional treatment of the central figure would have been less discordant with the truth and grandeur of the choruses.

The Saint as Tragic Hero: *Saint Joan* and *Murder in the Cathedral*

Louis L. Martz

The problem of the tragic writer in our day appears to be: how to control this threatened dissolution into mere pity of tragedy's double vision of suffering and affirmation, how to combine this "unreasoning sentiment" with something like the different vision that Santayana goes on to suggest: "Suppose now that I turn through the town gates and suddenly see a broad valley spread out before me with the purple sierra in the distance beyond. This expanse, this vastness, fills my intuition; also, perhaps, some sense of the deeper breath which I draw as if my breast expanded in sympathy with the rounded heavens." Thus we often find that the modern writer who seeks a tragic effect will attempt, by some device, such as Ibsen's family heritage or his view of the glacier, to give us the experience of a secret cause underlying his work of pity—to give it broader dimensions, sharper form, to render the ultimate objects distinguishable, to prevent it from spreading blindly outwards. We can see this plainly in O'Neill's *Mourning Becomes Electra,* where O'Neill, by borrowing from Aeschylus the ancient idea of a family curse, is able to give his drama a firm, stark outline and to endow his heroine with something like a tragic dignity. The only trouble is that this Freudian version of a family curse is not secret enough: it tends to announce itself hysterically, all over the place: "I'm

From *Tragic Themes in Western Literature,* edited by Cleanth Brooks. © 1955 by Louis L. Martz. Yale University Press, 1955.

the last Mannon. I've got to punish myself!" In the end we feel that this family curse has been shipped in from Greece and has never quite settled down in New England.

Eliot has described much the same difficulty which appears in his play *The Family Reunion,* where he too, even more boldly than O'Neill, has tried to borrow the Furies from Aeschylus. Eliot deploys his Furies, quite impolitely, in the middle of Ibsen's drawing room. As we might expect, they were not welcome: "We tried every possible manner of presenting them," says Eliot. "We put them on the stage, and they looked like uninvited guests who had strayed in from a fancy-dress ball. We concealed them behind gauze, and they suggested a still out of a Walt Disney film. We made them dimmer, and they looked like shrubbery just outside the window. I have seen other expedients tried": Eliot adds, "I have seen them signalling from across the garden, or swarming onto the stage like a football team, and they are never right. They never succeed in being either Greek goddesses or modern spooks. But their failure," he concludes, "is merely a symptom of the failure to adjust the ancient with the modern." Or, we might say, a failure to adjust the ancient Aeschylean symbol of a secret cause with the modern human sufferer.

How, then, can it be done? It is in their approach to this problem that *Saint Joan* and *Murder in the Cathedral* reveal their peculiar power, an approach that seems to have been made possible by this fact: that both Shaw and Eliot feel they cannot depend upon their audience to accept their saintly heroes as divinely inspired. The dramaturgy of both plays is based upon a deliberate manipulation of the elements of religious skepticism or uncertainty in the audience.

As Eliot's play moves toward the somber conclusion of its first half, the Four Tempters cry out in the temptation of self-pity ("It's just a dirty trick"):

> Man's life is a cheat and a disappointment
>
> . . . .
>
> All things become less real, man passes
> From unreality to unreality.
> This man [Becket] is obstinate, blind, intent
> On self-destruction,
> Passing from deception to deception,
> From grandeur to grandeur to final illusion.

And a page later the Chorus too cries out from the world of Ernest

Hemingway, with also, perhaps, a slight reminiscence of the millrace in *Rosmersholm:*

> We have seen the young man mutilated,
> The torn girl trembling by the mill-stream.
> And meanwhile we have gone on living,
> Living and partly living,
> Picking together the pieces,
> Gathering faggots at nightfall,
> Building a partial shelter,
> For sleeping, and eating and drinking and laughter.

And then, at the very close of part 1, Becket sums up the whole attitude when he turns sharply to address the audience:

> I know
> What yet remains to show you of my history
> Will seem to most of you at best futility,
> Senseless self-slaughter of a lunatic,
> Arrogant passion of a fanatic,
> I know that history at all times draws
> The strangest consequence from remotest cause.

It is exactly the challenge that Shaw has thrown at his readers in the preface to *Saint Joan:* "For us to set up our condition as a standard of sanity, and declare Joan mad because she never condescended to it, is to prove that we are not only lost but irredeemable."

Eliot and Shaw, then, seem to be assuming that the least touch of theology in their plays will serve—to raise a question. And so the saint may become a figure well adapted to arouse something very close to a tragic experience: for here the words sacred, glorious, sacrifice, and the expression in vain may become once again easily appropriate; while at the same time the uncertainty of the audience's attitude—and to some extent the dramatist's own—may enable him to deal also with the painful and pitiful aspects of experience that form the other side of the tragic tension.

But this conflict, this double vision, is not, in these plays, primarily contained within the figure of the saint as tragic hero: Joan and Becket do not here represent humanity in the way of Hamlet or King Oedipus —by focusing within themselves the full tragic tension. They are much more like Oedipus at Colonus, who, although a pitiful beggar in appearance, speaks now through the power of a superhuman insight.

Most of his mind lies beyond suffering: he feels that he has found the secret cause, and under the impulse of that cause he moves onward magnificently to his death and transfiguration. The sense of human suffering in *Oedipus at Colonus* is conveyed chiefly in retrospect, or in the sympathetic outcries of the chorus, the weeping of the rejected Polynices, and the anguish of the two daughters whom Oedipus must leave behind.

To see these plays as in any sense tragic it seems that we must abandon the concept of a play built upon an ideal Aristotelian hero and look instead for a tragic experience that arises from the interaction between a hero, who represents the secret cause, and the other characters, who represent the human sufferers. The point is brought out, ironically, by the Archbishop, near the end of Shaw's play, when he warns Joan against the sin of pride, saying, "The old Greek tragedy is rising among us. It is the chastisement of hubris." Joan replies with her usual bluntness, asking, "How can you say that I am disobedient when I always obey my voices, because they come from God." But when the Archbishop insists that "all the voices that come to you are the echoes of your own wilfulness," when he declares angrily, "You stand alone: absolutely alone, trusting to your own conceit, your own ignorance, your own headstrong presumption, your own impiety," we are reminded of Creon berating Oedipus at Colonus, and we are reminded too of Oedipus's long declaration of innocence when Joan turns away, "her eyes skyward," saying, "I have better friends and better counsel than yours."

There is nothing complex about the character of Shaw's Joan; it is the whole fabric of the play that creates something like a tragic tension. For whatever he may say in his preface, Shaw the dramatist, through his huge cast of varied human types, probes the whole range of belief and disbelief in Joan's voices. "They come from your imagination," says the feeble de Baudricourt in the opening scene. "Of course," says Joan, "That is how the messages of God come to us." Cauchon believes the girl to be "inspired, but diabolically inspired." "Many saints have said as much as Joan," Ladvenu suggests. Dunois, her only friend, senses some aura of divinity about her, but becomes extremely uneasy when she talks about her voices. "I should think," he says, "you were a bit cracked if I hadn't noticed that you give me very sensible reasons for what you do, though I hear you telling others you are only obeying Madame Saint Catherine." "Well," she replies, "I have to find reasons for you, because you do not believe in my voices. But the voices come

first; and I find the reasons after: whatever you may choose to believe."
Whatever you may choose to believe: there is the point, and as the figure of
Joan flashes onward through the play with only one lapse in confidence—her brief recantation—Shaw keeps his play hovering among
choices in a highly modern state of uncertainty: we know and do not
know: until at the close Shaw seems to send us over on the side of affirmation. We agree, at least, with the words of the French captain in the
opening scene: "There is something about her. . . . Something. . . . I
think the girl herself is a bit of a miracle."

She is, as Eliot would say, "a white light still and moving," the
simple *cause* of every other word and action in the play; and her absolute simplicity of vision cuts raspingly through all the malign or well-
intentioned errors of the world, until in its wrath the world rises up in
the form of all its assembled institutions and declares by the voice of all
its assembled doctors that this girl is—as Shaw says—*insufferable.*

Thus Joan's apparent resemblance to the Aristotelian hero: her
extreme self-confidence, her brashness, her appearance of rash impet-
uosity—all this becomes in the end a piece of Shavian irony, for her
only real error in the play is the one point where her superb self-
confidence breaks down in the panic of recantation. And so the hubris
is not Joan's but Everyman's. The characters who accuse Joan of pride
and error are in those accusations convicting themselves of the pride of
self-righteousness and the errors of human certitude. It is true that the
suffering that results from this pride and error remains in Shaw's play
rather theoretical and remote: and yet we feel it in some degree: in the
pallor and anguish of Joan as she resists the temptation to doubt her
voices, in the rather unconvincing screams of De Stogumber at the
close, and, much more effectively, in the quiet, controlled sympathy of
Ladvenu. It would seem, then, that some degree of tragedy resides in
this failure of Everyman to recognize absolute Reality, the secret cause,
when it appears in the flesh. Must then, cries Cauchon in the epilogue,
"Must then a Christ perish in torment in every age to save those that
have no imagination?" It is the same symbolism that Eliot has evoked
in the beginning of his play, where the Chorus asks: "Shall the Son of
Man be born again in the litter of scorn?"

We need not be too greatly concerned with Shaw's bland asser-
tions that he is letting us in on the truth about the Middle Ages, telling
us in the play all we need to know about Joan. Books and articles have
appeared—a whole cloudburst of them—devoted to proving that
Shaw's methods of historical research in his play and in his preface are

open to serious question. But Shaw gave that game away long ago when he announced: "I deal with all periods; but I never study any period but the present, which I have not yet mastered and never shall"; or when he said, with regard to Cleopatra's cure for Caesar's baldness, that his methods of scholarship, as compared with Gilbert Murray's, consisted in "pure divination." The preface to *Saint Joan* lays down a long barrage of historicity, which in the end is revealed as a remarkable piece of Shavio-Swiftian hoaxing: for in the last few pages of that long preface he adds, incidentally, that his use of the "available documentation" has been accompanied by "such powers of divination as I possess"; he concedes that for some figures in his play he has invented "appropriate characters" "in Shakespear's manner"; and that, fundamentally, his play is built upon what he calls "the inevitable flatteries of tragedy." That is, there is no historical basis for his highly favorable characterizations of Cauchon and the Inquisitor, upon which the power and point of the trial scene are founded.

I do not mean to say, however, that our sense of history is irrelevant to an appreciation of Shaw's play. There is a point to be made by considering such a book as J. M. Robertson's *Mr. Shaw and "The Maid,"* which complains bitterly, upon historical grounds, against Shaw's "instinct to put things both ways." This is a book, incidentally, which Eliot has praised very highly because it points out that in this kind of subject "Facts matter," and that "to Mr. Shaw, truth and falsehood . . . do not seem to have the same meaning as to ordinary people." But the point lies rather in the tribute that such remarks pay to the effectiveness of Shaw's realistic dramaturgy.

Shaw is writing, as he and Ibsen had to write, within the conventions of the modern realistic theater—conventions which Eliot escaped in *Murder in the Cathedral* because he was writing this play for performance at the Canterbury Festival. But in his later plays, composed for the theater proper, Eliot has also been forced to, at least he has chosen to, write within these stern conventions.

Now in the realistic theater, as Francis Fergusson has suggested, the artist seems to be under the obligation to pretend that he is not an artist at all but is simply interested in pursuing the truth "in some pseudo-scientific sense." Thus we find the relation of art to life so often driven home on the modern stage by such deep symbolic actions as removing the cubes from ice trays or cooking an omelette for dinner. Shaw knows that on this stage facts matter—or at least the appearance of facts—and in this need for a dramatic realism lies the basic justification for Shaw's elaborately argued presentation of Joan as a Protestant and nationalist martyr killed by the combined institutional forces of feudalism and the Church. Through these historical theories, developed within the body of the play, Joan is presented as the agent of a transformation in the actual world; the theories have enough plausibility for dramatic purposes, and perhaps a bit more; this, together with Shaw's adaptation of the records of Joan's trial, gives him all the "facts" that he needs to make his point in the modern theater.

Some of Joan's most Shavian remarks are in fact her own words as set down in the long records of her trial: as, for example, where her questioner asks whether Michael does not appear to her as a naked man. "Do you think God cannot afford clothes for him?" answers Joan, in the play and in the records. Shaw has made a skillful selection of these answers, using, apparently, the English translation of the documents edited by Douglas Murray; and he has set these answers together with speeches of his own modeled upon their tone and manner. In this way he has been able to bring within the limits of the realistic theater the very voice that rings throughout these trial records, the voice of the lone girl fencing with, stabbing at, baffling, and defeating the crowd of some sixty learned men: a voice that is not speaking within the range of the other voices that assail her. Thus we hear her in the following speech adapted from half a dozen places in the records: "I have said again and again that I will tell you all that concerns this trial. But I cannot tell you the whole truth: God does not allow the whole truth to be told. . . . It is an old saying that he who tells too much truth is sure to be hanged. . . . I have sworn as much as I will swear; and I will swear no more." Or, following the documents much more closely, her answers thus resound when the questioners attempt to force her to submit her case to the Church on earth: "I will obey The Church," says Joan, "provided it does not command anything impossible."

> If you command me to declare that all I have done and said, and all the visions and revelations I have had, were not from God, then that is impossible: I will not declare it for anything in the world. What God made me do I will never go back on; and what He has commanded or shall command I will not fail to do in spite of any man alive. That is what I mean by impossible. And in case The Church should bid me do anything contrary to the command I have from God, I will not consent to it, no matter what it may be.

In thus maintaining the tone of that—extraordinary—voice, Shaw has, I think, achieved an effect that is in some ways very close to the effect of the "intersection of the timeless with time," which Eliot has achieved in his play, and which he has described in "The Dry Salvages":

> Men's curiosity searches past and future
> And clings to that dimension. But to apprehend
> The point of intersection of the timeless
> With time, is an occupation for the saint—
> No occupation either, but something given
> And taken, in a lifetime's death in love,
> Ardour and selflessness and self-surrender.

An obvious similarity between the two plays may be seen in the tone of satirical wit that runs through both—notably in the ludicrous prose speeches that Eliot's murdering Knights deliver to the audience in self-defense. These have an essentially Shavian purpose: "to shock the audience out of their complacency," as Eliot has recently said, going on to admit, "I may, for aught I know, have been slightly under the influence of *St. Joan*" ("Poetry and Drama"). The atmosphere of wit is evident also in the first part of Eliot's play, in the cynical attitude of the Herald who announces Becket's return:

> The streets of the city will be packed to suffocation,
> And I think that his horse will be deprived of its tail,
> A single hair of which becomes a precious relic.

Or, more important, in the speeches of the Four Tempters, who match the Four Knights of part 2, and who tend to speak, as the Knights also do in places, in a carefully calculated doggerel that betrays their fundamental shallowness:

> I leave you to the pleasures of your higher vices,
> Which will have to be paid for at higher prices.
> Farewell, my Lord, I do not wait upon ceremony,
> I leave as I came, forgetting all acrimony,
> Hoping that your present gravity
> Will find excuse for my humble levity.
> If you will remember me, my Lord, at your prayers,
> I'll remember you at kissing-time below the stairs.

In all these ways Eliot, like Shaw, maintains his action in the "real" world: and by other means as well. By keeping before us the central question of our own time: "Is it war or peace?" asks Eliot's priest. "Peace," replies the Herald, "but not the kiss of peace. / A patched up affair, if you ask my opinion." By the frequently realistic imagery of the Chorus, made up of "the scrubbers and sweepers of Canterbury." By the frequent use in part 2 of the recorded words that passed between Becket and the Knights in the year 1170. By throwing our minds back to the literary forms of the Middle Ages: to *Everyman,* from which Eliot has taken a good many hints for the tone and manner of Becket's encounter with the Tempters, and which, as he says, he has kept in mind as a model for the versification of his dialogue. To this last we should also add a special device of heavy alliteration (particularly notable in the Second Temptation), which seems to work in two ways: it reminds us of the English alliterative verse of the Middle Ages, and thus gives the play a further historical focus, and it also suggests here a rhetoric of worldly ambition in keeping with the temptation that Becket is undergoing:

> Think, my lord,
> Power obtained grows to glory,
> Life lasting, a permanent possession,
> A templed tomb, monument of marble.
> Rule over men reckon no madness.

Both Eliot and Shaw, then, have in their own ways taken pains to place their action simultaneously in the "real" past and the "real" present: an action firmly fixed in time must underlie the shock of intersection.

But of course in Eliot's play the cause of intersection, the agent of transformation, the saint, is utterly different from Shaw's, and thus the plays become, so obviously, different. Shaw's Joan is the active saint, operating in the world; Eliot's Becket is a contemplative figure, ascetic, "withdrawn to contemplation," holding within his mind, and reconciling there alone, the stresses of the world. His immobility is his strength; he is the still point, the center of the world that moves about him, as his sermon is the center of the play.

One is struck here by the similarity between the total conception of Eliot's play and of *Oedipus at Colonus.* Both heroes, after a long period of wandering, have found, at their entrance, their place of rest and their place of death in a sacred spot: Becket in his Cathedral, Oedipus in the sacred wood of the Furies or Eumenides. Both heroes maintain the attitude that Oedipus states at the outset: "Nevermore will I depart from my rest in this land." Both reveal in their opening speeches the view that, as Oedipus says, "patience is the lesson of suffering." Both are then subjected to various kinds of temptations to leave the spot; both are forced to recapitulate their past while enduring these trials; both remain immobile, unmovable; both win a glorious death and by that death benefit the land in which they die. Both are surrounded by a large cast of varied human sufferers, who do not understand the saint, who try to deflect him from his ways, and who in some cases mourn his loss bitterly: the cry of Eliot's priest at the end is like the cries of Antigone and Ismene:

> O father, father, gone from us, lost to us,
> How shall we find you, from what far place
> Do you look down on us?

I suspect that *Oedipus at Colonus* has in fact had a deep and early influence upon Eliot's whole career: "Sweeney among the Nightingales" alludes to this very wood, which Sophocles' chorus describes as a place where

> The sweet, sojourning nightingale
> Murmurs all day long.
>
> . . . .
>
> And here the choiring Muses come,
> And the divinity of love
> With the gold reins in her hand.

The fact that the Muses haunt this wood may throw some light too upon the title of Eliot's first book of essays, *The Sacred Wood,* the book in which he revealed his early interest in the possibility of a poetic drama.

But our main point here is the way in which this deeply religious tragedy of Sophocles, which had already provided a strong formative precedent for Milton's *Samson Agonistes,* now provides us with a precedent for regarding Eliot's saint's play as a tragedy. The precedent may also explain why a strong coloring of Greek-like fatalism runs throughout Eliot's Christian play: a coloring which some of Eliot's critics have found disturbing. But these classical reminiscences of Destiny and Fate and Fortune's wheel remind us only of the base upon which Eliot is building: they do not delimit his total meaning. We can see this amalgamation of Greek and Christian at work in Becket's opening speech—the most important speech of the play, which all the rest of the play explores and illustrates. It is the speech which Becket's

Fourth Tempter, his inmost self, repeats in mockery, word for word, twenty pages later and thus suggests that these Temptations—of pleasure, worldly power, and spiritual pride—are to be regarded as fundamentally a recapitulation of the stages by which Becket has reached the state of mind he displays at his entrance. He believes that he has found a secret cause, and he enters prepared to die in that belief: "Peace," he says to the worried priest, and then, referring to the Chorus of anxious women, continues:

> They speak better than they know, and beyond your
>   understanding
> They know and do not know, what it is to act or suffer.
> They know and do not know, that acting is suffering
> And suffering is action. Neither does the actor suffer
> Nor the patient act. But both are fixed
> In an eternal action, an eternal patience
> To which all must consent that it may be willed
> And which all must suffer that they may will it,
> That the pattern may subsist, for the pattern is the action
> And the suffering, that the wheel may turn and still
> Be forever still.

We can worry about the ambiguities of those words "suffering" and "patient" as long as we wish: in the end Becket keeps his secret almost as stubbornly as Joan or Oedipus:

> I have had a tremor of bliss, a wink of heaven, a whisper,
> And I would no longer be denied; all things
> Proceed to a joyful consummation.

But halfway between these two passages lies Becket's Christmas sermon, presented as a four-page interlude between the play's two parts. It is one of the most surprisingly successful moments in the modern theater, for who would expect to find a sermon, and an interesting sermon, here? It owes its success to an atmosphere of restrained and controlled mystery and to the fact that it is not really an interlude at all, but a deep expression of the play's central theme, binding the play's two parts into one. Becket is speaking of this word *Peace*, the word that dominates the play, for all the actors and sufferers in the play are seeking peace, on their own terms. But the meaning of the word for Becket is conveyed only obliquely, by Becket's tone, his poise, his humility, his acceptance, "Thus devoted, concentrated in purpose." He can display only by his own action and suffering what this word Peace means to him, for he is trying to explain the meaning of the unspoken Word that lies locked in the visible and verbal paradoxes of acting and suffering.

And only in this way, too, can Becket display that submission of the will by which he avoids the final temptation of spiritual pride. The Temptations make it clear that Becket has been a proud man—even an arrogant man: the first priest, the Tempters, and the Knights all accuse him, with some reason, of pride. And we hear him speaking at times throughout the play, and even at the very end, in a harsh, acid tone, which here and there is uncomfortably close to condescension. Eliot's control of the character is not perhaps as firm as we could wish, though there is nothing that a skillful actor cannot handle, for the central conception is clear: like Oedipus, Becket is still a man, and retains the marks of his natural character: but in the sermon we grasp his saintliness.

At the same time Becket conveys to us the essence of the view of Tragedy that we are here considering. Becket's sermon ponders the fact that in the services of Christmas the Church celebrates birth and death simultaneously. Now, "as the World sees," Becket says, "this is to behave in a strange fashion. For who in the World will both mourn and rejoice at once and for the same reason?" And this is true on other occasions, he adds: "so also, in a smaller figure, we both rejoice and mourn in the death of martyrs. We mourn, for the sins of the world that has martyred them; we rejoice, that another soul is numbered among the Saints."

It is this tension, this double vision, that Eliot presents in his great choral odes. What Eliot has done is to allow everyone in his play except the Chorus and Becket to remain the simplest possible types—simpler even than Shaw's: ciphers who serve their functions: to provide an outline of the action and a setting for the problem. Into the cries of the Chorus he has poured the tragic experience of suffering humanity, caught in the grip of a secret cause: "We are forced to bear witness."

The Chorus opens the play with fear and reluctance and hopelessness, asking who it is who shall

> Stretch out his hand to the fire, and deny his master?
> Who shall be warm
> By the Fire, and deny his master?

They know and do not know who it is—themselves—bending to the earth like animals seeking their protective coloring:

> Now I fear disturbance of the quiet seasons:
> Winter shall come bringing death from the sea,
> Ruinous spring shall beat at our doors,
> Root and shoot shall eat our eyes and our ears,
> Disastrous summer burn up the beds of our streams
> And the poor shall wait for another decaying October.

These dead do not desire resurrection; and when their Lord Arch-bishop reappears to them, they can only cry out, "O Thomas, return, Archbishop; return, return to France. . . . Leave us to perish in quiet." They would like to go on "living and partly living," like Shaw's Dauphin, who irritably shies away from Joan, saying, "I want to sleep in a comfortable bed." Eliot's Chorus starts from this point—by the fireside and the bed—a point which Shaw's chorus of varied actors hardly goes beyond. But Eliot's Chorus moves far beyond this point, undergoing what Kenneth Burke or Francis Fergusson might call a ritual of transformation. They are not at all the "foolish, immodest and babbling women," which Eliot's priest calls them, but the heart of humanity moving under the impulse of a half-realized cause. Under this impulse they have moved, by the end of part 1, into the range of a "stifling scent of despair," which nevertheless is not spreading blindly outwards: for the Chorus

> The forms take shape in the dark air:
> Puss-purr of leopard, footfall of padding bear,
> Palm-pat of nodding ape, square hyaena waiting
> For laughter, laughter, laughter. The Lords of Hell are here.

But after Becket's sermon the Chorus has taken some heart: they no longer seem to fear the spring:

> When the leaf is out on the tree, when the elder and may
> Burst over the stream, and the air is clear and high,
> And voices trill at windows, and children tumble in front of
>   the door,
> What work shall have been done, what wrong
> Shall the bird's song cover, the green tree cover, what
>   wrong
> Shall the fresh earth cover?

From this oscillation between despair and a half-hope arises the play's greatest poetry, as the Chorus moves on far out of the range of

ordinary fears and hopes into a nightmare vision that renews and ex-
tends the animal imagery and the dense imagery of taste and smell and
the other senses, by which the Chorus had expressed its horror at the
close of part 1; but now there is more than horror: the Chorus is moving on here to a vision of humanity's living relation with all being, to a
sense that all of creation from the worm to the Prince is involved in this
sacrifice:

> I have smelt them, the death-bringers, senses are quickened
> By subtile forebodings
>
> . . . .
>
>   I have tasted
> The savour of putrid flesh in the spoon. I have felt
> The heaving of earth at nightfall, restless, absurd. I have
>   heard
> Laughter in the noises of beasts that make strange noises
>
> . . . .
>
>   I have eaten
> Smooth creatures still living, with the strong salt taste of
>   living things under sea
>
> . . . .
>
>   In the air
> Flirted with the passage of the kite, I have plunged with the
>   kite and cowered with the wren.
>
> . . . .
>
>   I have seen
> Rings of light coiling downwards, descending
> To the horror of the ape.
>
> . . . .
>
> I have consented, Lord Archbishop, have consented.

Beyond this recognition of responsibility for the action and the suffering, there lies a step into the vision of ultimate horror which they face
just before the murder: a vision of utter spiritual death: the Dark Night
of the Soul:

> Emptiness, absence, separation from God;
> The horror of the effortless journey, to the empty land
> Which is no land, only emptiness, absence, the Void.

This, paradoxically, is their moment of deepest vision, of greatest
courage; the point at which they fully comprehend their need for the

sacrifice about to be permitted, suffered, and which provides the answer to their cries during the very act of the murder: "Clear the air!
clean the sky! wash the wind! take the stone from the stone, take the
skin from the arm, take the muscle from the bone, and wash them.
Wash the stone, wash the bone, wash the brain, wash the soul, wash
them wash them!" Like King Oedipus they are, without quite realiz-
ing it, being washed in this "rain of blood" that is blinding their eyes.

As these cries from the conscience of humanity fade away, the
lights fade out—and then come on again in the foreground with a
glaring brightness—as the four Murderers step forward, make their
bows, and present their ridiculous speeches of defense—in the manner
of an after-dinner speaker: "I knew Becket well, in various official
relations; and I may say that I have never known a man so well quali-
fied for the highest rank of the Civil Service." Or in the manner of the
parliamentary orator: "I must repeat one point that the last speaker has
made. While the late Archbishop was Chancellor, he wholeheartedly
supported the King's designs: this is an important point, which, if
necessary, I can substantiate." Or in the manner of the brisk attorney:
"I think, with these facts before you, you will unhesitatingly render a
verdict of Suicide while of Unsound Mind."

The lights fade out again, the Knights disappear, and then gradually
the lights come on once more to reveal the priests and the Chorus in their
old positions. It is as if the Knights had never spoken: the conscience of
humanity has been working deep within while the Knights were speaking on the surface, and now the Chorus sums up its discoveries, its transformation, in a psalm of praise, in which once again it affirms a union
with the whole creation, but this time in a tone of joy and peace:

> We praise Thee, O God, for Thy glory displayed in all the
> creatures of the earth,
> In the snow, in the rain, in the wind, in the storm; in all of
> Thy creatures, both the hunters and the hunted.
>
> . . . .
>
> They affirm Thee in living; all things affirm Thee in living;
> the bird in the air, both the hawk and the finch; the
> beast on the earth, both the wolf and the lamb; the
> worm in the soil and the worm in the belly.
>
> . . . .
>
> Even in us the voices of seasons, the snuffle of winter, the
> song of spring, the drone of summer, the voices of
> beasts and of birds, praise Thee.

Those words from the final chorus may remind us again of the long tentacles of correlated imagery that reach throughout these choral odes: imagery of beasts and birds and worms; of seasons, of violent death, of the daily hardships of the partly living life: with the result that these choral odes grow together into a long poem, interwoven with verse and prose pitched at a lower intensity; and by this interweaving of the odes, even more than by Becket, the play is drawn into unity.

We can see now the effect that these different manifestations of a secret cause have had upon the total construction of our two saint's plays. Eliot's play, focused on a contemplative saint, displays what we might call a semicircular structure: with Becket as the still center and the Chorus sweeping out around him in a broad dramatic action, a poetical ballet of transformation. Shaw's play, based on an active saint, develops instead a linear structure, as of a spear driving straight for the mark. It is marred, here and there, by irrelevant or maladjusted witticisms, and the whole character of De Stogumber is a misfortune. Yet Joan and her voices seem to work like key symbols in a poem: appearing in a carefully designed sequence of different contexts: six scenes, with six differing moods, moving from farce to high comedy, to a romantic glimpse of the warrior Joan in shining armor, and from here into an area of deepening somberness, until, by the fifth scene, the world of Shaw's play, too, has been transformed—from the foolish to the tragic. Now we have in his play, too, the dim silence of the Cathedral, with Joan praying symbolically before the Stations of the Cross: her white raiment revealing the saint whose mission is now nearly complete. The king is crowned; she has shown France how to win; and now, as her allies, one by one, and even Dunois, fail to answer the unbearable demands of the superhuman, Joan goes forth to meet the cheering crowd who will kiss her garments and line her roadway with palms. The way is now prepared for the massive trial scene, the tragic agon, which presents what Eliot calls "a symbol perfected in death."

And then, the epilogue. Many have found this a disconcerting, inartistic mixture of farce, satire, and didactic explanation. I agree. But I do not see why the epilogue should spoil the play. An epilogue is no part of the dramatic action: it is the author's chance to step forward, relaxed and garrulous, and to talk the play over with the audience. Traditionally, it is true, the epilogue is recited by only one performer—by Prospero, for instance. There is a slight difference here: Shaw has had his entire cast recite the epilogue. But it is still appended commentary on the action, not a part of the action. Moreover, this kind of thing is not without precedent in performances of tragedy. The ancient Greeks appear to have liked exactly this kind of release in their festivals of tragedy, since they demanded that each dramatist, after presenting his three tragedies, should provide them with their satyr-play, usually of an uproarious and ribald variety, sometimes burlesquing elements of the very story that had just been seen in tragic dignity. The epilogue is Shaw's satyr-play: a bursting forth of that strong sense of the ridiculous which Shaw has, during the play proper, subjected to a remarkable control—remarkable, that is, for Shaw.

It seems possible, then, to find some place, within the spacious area of tragedy, for our two saint's plays. It seems possible, if we will not demand an Aristotelian hero, and if we may view the area of tragedy as a sort of scale or spectrum ranging between the two poles of doubt and affirmation: or, to put it more precisely, between the pole of fruitless suffering and the pole of universal cause. Not a scale of value, but a spectrum of various qualities, with *A Farewell to Arms* marking one extreme, outside the area of tragedy, and Shakespeare's *Tempest,* perhaps, marking the other extreme. In between, within the area of tragedy, would lie an enormous variety of works that would defy any rigorous attempt at definition, except that all would show in some degree a mingled atmosphere of doubt and affirmation, of human suffering and secret cause. Far over toward the side of fruitless suffering we might find the plays of Ibsen, or *Othello;* somewhere in the middle, *Hamlet,* or *Oedipus Rex;* and far over toward the other side we might find a triad of strongly affirmative tragedies: *Oedipus at Colonus, Samson Agonistes,* and *Murder in the Cathedral;* and still farther over, perhaps hanging on by his hands to the very rim of tragedy—we might even find a place for Bernard Shaw.

The New Rhythm

Carol H. Smith

Murder in the Cathedral was written for the Canterbury Festival of June 1935 and, although Eliot was apparently given complete freedom to submit what he pleased, the limitations of a subject appropriate to the festival's purpose and an audience which was expecting a religious drama were nevertheless present.

One instructive glimpse into Eliot's thinking on the subject of his commission by the Canterbury Festival Committee and the whole matter of "Christian propaganda" is provided by an article written for "Notes on the Way" during the composition of the play. He observes that the artist who employs his abilities in the service of a cause does so at his own risk,

> For one danger is that the cause may not be big enough, or profound and permanent enough, not to become somewhat ridiculous under such treatment; and another danger is that you will not succeed in transmuting it into a personal and peculiar passion. The making of great poetry requires a just and delicate sense of values; distorted or incomplete values may easily turn the sublime into the ridiculous. . . . I question whether any of the social causes agitated in our time is complete enough to provide much food for poetry.

The implication of this statement seems to be that while none of the social causes of his time were complete enough for the great poet, the artist committed to values of unquestionable completeness and truth

---

From *T. S. Eliot's Dramatic Theory and Practice.* © 1963 by Princeton University Press.

41

would not face this difficulty. For the Christian artist, then, propaganda for his cause ceased to be partial and partisan, and became instead a complete and profound interpretation of life which made art possible. Eliot's comment in the same essay that St. Thomas of Canterbury might have preferred as Introit for his Feast day "Princes, moreover, did sit and did witness falsely against me," indicates that Eliot saw in the events leading to the martyrdom of Thomas Becket a situation involving the conflict between the church and world analogous to the modern struggle of the church against its enemies.

Far from giving up the idea of levels in the play's structure, Eliot made perhaps his most effective use of this conception in *Murder in the Cathedral.* The surface level of the action, dealing with the martyrdom of Becket, is divided into two parts which are connected by the "interlude" of the Archbishop's sermon on Christmas morning. In the opening chorus, the women of Canterbury express their desire to maintain the quiet sterility of their humble lives, undisturbed by greatness of any kind, "living and partly living." Their presentiment that the return of the Archbishop after his seven years' absence is near and that his return will bring a spiritual as well as a temporal disturbance in their lives fills them with terror. The women are conscious of fear, and desire only "peace" as they understand it; they "do not wish anything to happen." They are only intuitively aware of the greatness of the event—"Destiny waits in the hand of God, shaping the still unshapen."

The reaction of the three priests to the news of Thomas's return represents the next step on an ascending scale of awareness of the event's meaning. Their reactions begin where the women's leave off; they even begin by repeating some of the women's phrases. Within the group of priests, there is also a hierarchy of understanding. The First Priest, knowing his Archbishop's uncompromising nature, fears Thomas's return—"I fear for the Archbishop, I fear for the Church." The Second Priest affirms his loyalty to the Archbishop and sees in his strength a "rock" of God which will dispel "dismay and doubt." He differs from the women in wishing the return but he does not think beyond the comfort of Thomas's presence. It is the Third Priest who, of the three, most nearly approaches Thomas's saintly understanding of the events to come. He says, in language Thomas himself later uses, "For good or ill, let the wheel turn."

In the hierarchy of understanding presented by the characters in part 1, Thomas, of course, stands at the top, although even he is to reach a greater height by the conclusion of his temptations. When

Thomas enters and chides the Second Priest for scolding the women, he expresses in his first speech the message of the drama, a message which, when repeated to him later by one of his tempters, takes on a new meaning even for Thomas:

> They know and do not know, that acting is suffering
> And suffering is action. Neither does the actor suffer
> Nor the patient act. But both are fixed
> In an eternal action, an eternal patience
> To which all must consent that it may be willed
> And which all must suffer that they may will it,
> That the pattern may subsist, for the pattern is the action
> And the suffering, that the wheel may turn and still
> Be forever still.

This passage introduces both the action–suffering theme and the imagery of the wheel and the point.

Thomas also answers each of his four tempters in terms of his opening statement. When the First Tempter offers Thomas a return to the life of sensual pleasures of his youth at court, his reply is:

> Only
> The fool, fixed in his folly, may think
> He can turn the wheel on which he turns.

The Second Tempter offers earthly power with which to improve the temporal world and urges Thomas to seek power for present good and to leave holiness to the hereafter. Thomas replies that he serves the higher power of the Pope and a higher order than the world knows:

> Those who put their faith in worldly order
> Not controlled by the order of God,
> In confident ignorance, but arrest disorder,
> Make is fast, breed fatal disease,
> Degrade what they exalt.

The Third Tempter offers Thomas both revenge upon the King and domination for the Pope if he will side with the English barons—"Kings will allow no power but their own," thus "Church and people have good cause against the throne." Thomas replies:

> To make, then break, this thought has come before,
> The desperate exercise of failing power

> Samson in Gaza did no more.
> But if I break, I must break myself alone.

The Archbishop thus reveals the contradiction in his thinking. He thinks that he is rejecting the temptation of willing "action" by removing himself from the act of vengeance or of seeking power, but his statement reveals that by "willing" his own destruction he is committing an act incompatible with making his will compliant with God's. The repetition of "I" and the use of "myself alone" in the last line of Thomas's reply carry home this contradiction. At this point the Fourth Tempter enters and his mocking response to the Archbishop's comment is an excellent piece of dramatic irony: "Well done, Thomas, your will is hard to bend."

The Fourth Tempter offers first the power of martyrdom—"Saint and Martyr rule from the tomb"—and then the glory of "dwelling forever in presence of God" as a saint. He urges Thomas to:

> Seek the way of martyrdom, make yourself the lowest
> On earth, to be high in heaven.

When the Fourth Tempter repeats to Thomas his own words to the women, he realizes his error at last, that the pride of willing martyrdom is "the greatest treason: To do the right deed for the wrong reason." To "act" in such a way would be to try to turn the wheel himself, rather than to allow the "will" of the unmoved mover to rule. Part 1 ends with Thomas's address to the audience, a device later duplicated with an opposite motive by the Knights at the end of Part 2:

> But for every evil, every sacrilege,
> Crime, wrong, oppression and the axe's edge,
> Indifference, exploitation, you, and you,
> And you, must all be punished. So must you.
> I shall no longer act or suffer, to the sword's end.
> Now my good Angel, whom God appoints
> To be my guardian, hover over the swords' points.

Thomas is saying, in effect, that having endured his temptations and having reaffirmed submission to God's will and the divine pattern, he has moved beyond action and suffering, but that the rest of humanity, those too much a part of this world's desires, must endure the suffering implicit in action *and* the responsibility.

The prose "interlude" which separates the two parts of the play is

Thomas's sermon in the Cathedral on Christmas morning. The sermon's text, "Glory to God in the highest, and on earth peace, good will toward men" (Luke 2:14), is packed with implication, following as it does the action of part 1. Part 1 has shown the kinds of worldly glory Thomas has been offered and the kind he has chosen, the glory of God in the highest. The word "peace," also Thomas's first word in the play, has taken on the new significance of the state of the martyr who is beyond action and suffering, and "good will toward men" now has the double import of the martyr's forgiveness of his murderers, and his beneficent influence with God for those who pray for his intercession. The juxtaposition of "God in the highest, and on earth" also suggests the high-low imagery of the wheel. It is, moreover, appropriate that the saint who goes soon to glory should echo the message of the heavenly host to the shepherds at Bethlehem.

In the sermon itself Thomas points out the special significance of the Christmas Mass; it is both the celebration of the joy of Christ's birth and the sorrow of His death. Thomas differentiates God's peace from peace as the world knows it and draws the analogy between Christ and the martyr. He closes the sermon with his newly won insight into martyrdom—that the martyr is not made by his own design but by God's.

In the first published editions of the play, part 2 opened with the entrance of the three Priests carrying the banners of St. Stephen, St. John the Apostle, and the Holy Innocents, and accompanied by the Introits of St. Stephen and St. John. The device was obviously an attempt to unify the time sequence—each banner representing one day which had passed since Christmas—as well as to show the significance of saints and martyrs in the church year and to foreshadow Thomas's own fate of martyrdom. In later versions the opening was replaced by the choral reaction of the women to the Archbishop's sermon. Their earlier fear of the spring and of a spiritual awakening has changed to an attitude nearer acceptance.

When the Knights enter they display, in their appearance and demeanor, a bestiality which is intended to contrast with the mildness and hospitality of the Priests. Their violence symbolizes the animality of man when he does not comply with God's will, but exercises his own instead. In man's desire for freedom from the moral restraints of a higher order, he condemns himself unwittingly to the tyranny of his passions. When Thomas appears the Knights demand to see him alone. They hurl insults at him, ridiculing his humble origins and accusing him of disloyalty to the King and of acting as he has because of ambition and pride. Thomas's reply is that he has always been a loyal vassal to the King: "Saving my order, I am at his command." His comment emphasizes the point that in clinging to the church over the King he is both saving and being saved by his order, which is God's order. His reply also suggests that the man of God is the only really loyal vassal, for all loyalty and morality must be based on divine order. This meaning is enforced when Thomas accuses the Knights of being disloyal themselves and demands that their accusations be made publicly. The angered Knights begin to attack him but are restrained when the Priests and attendants quickly return. The argument which follows explores the meaning of loyalty and treason. The Knights outline the King's grievances—that Thomas had put the King in disfavor with the Pope, that even after being pardoned by the King and reinstated, Thomas had suspended those who had crowned the young prince and denied the legality of his coronation. Thomas insists that he had only acted on the instructions of the Pope and that only the Pope could absolve the bishops. The Knights announce that they bring the King's command that Thomas be exiled but the Archbishop refuses to leave. The Knights depart in a fury, hurling accusations of treason and treachery. To their threats to return Thomas answers that he is ready for martyrdom.

The reaction of the women to the approaching murder is impassioned and even hysterical. Their acceptance of their share of the guilt, echoing Thomas's earlier statement to the audience that all must partake and suffer for such an act, shows that they have arrived at the stage of Christian responsibility, but their passion also indicates that they cannot yet accept or perceive God's will with quietness:

> I have consented, Lord Archbishop, have consented.
> Am torn away, subdued, violated,
> United to the spiritual flesh of nature,
> Mastered by the animal powers of spirit,
> Dominated by the lust of self-demolition,
> By the final utter uttermost death of spirit,
> By the final ecstasy of waste and shame.

Thomas comforts the women with the message that they will afterward see the glory of the act which they now witness in horror.

The Priests urge Thomas to flee or hide but he refuses, insisting that he will meet death gladly if it is God's will, but the now-frantic Priests succeed in dragging him off to vespers. The desire for action by the Priests shows that even they have not understood God's will. In the hierarchy of characters only Thomas, who is at the still center of the wheel of action and suffering, experiences peace.

In the Cathedral the Priests have barred the door, but Thomas demands that "the church shall be open, even to our enemies." When the Priests exclaim that these are not men but maddened beasts who attack him, Thomas admonishes them that they argue as the world argues, not as God does. The doors are opened and the Knights enter, maddened with drink, and taunt Thomas in a jazz chant which resembles Vachel Lindsay's "Daniel Jazz," one of the few remaining echoes of *Sweeney Agonistes* in this play. While the chorus demands a cleansing of the impure world, Thomas is slain by the Knights, who circle around him with outstretched swords, visually forming for the audience a wheel with Thomas as the still point.

The playwright's concern to communicate his message to the audience is evident in many aspects of the play. The full involvement of the chorus in Thomas's martyrdom, for example, is intended to enable the audience to observe their own representative group, "the type of the common man," travel the Christian path. The author hoped that those in the audience unable to identify with Thomas could perhaps identify with the women of Canterbury. While Eliot's esteem for the common man has never been high, in his conception of the chorus in *Murder in the Cathedral* he adopted a view at least more complimentary than that which he held when he wrote *Sweeney Agonistes,* when he felt that the majority of the audience would be incapable of sharing any response except that of the visionless and materialistic characters of that play. At least, the chorus has come to an understanding on their own level which can involve them in salvation.

The final appearance of the Knights just before the end of the play is another attempt to establish contact with the modern audience. The Knights address the audience in the contemporary prose of political debate. Eliot's avowed intent was "to shock the audience out of their complacency" and according to E. Martin Browne's account [in "From *The Rock* to *The Confidential Clerk*"] of the 1935 production that effect was certainly achieved. The Knights defend their actions on several grounds and according to the best modern logic. They insist that they were disinterested, that violence was the only way to secure social justice, and that Thomas's death should ultimately be judged "suicide while of unsound mind." The modernity of the language and argumentation is presumably to emphasize the kind of judgment on martyrdom which the modern secular world would approve—and to convince the audience of the blasphemy of that view.

The insertion of the prose of modern debate in the normally poetic and religious texture of the play is also intended, I believe, to point up the contrast between the "poetry" of the Catholic view of life, in the sense of its order and "rhythm," and the "prose" quality of the disordered, chaotic, and utilitarian materialism of modern existence. The mixture of dramatic moods produced by this device also constitutes a new use of Eliot's earlier ideas on the value of mixing the comic and the tragic in order to arrive at a more fundamental interpretation of events than either genre can afford. Thus the events in *Murder in the Cathedral* are presented as neither tragic nor comic, but Christian, for Thomas goes to glory although he suffers martyrdom. In Eliot's conception of drama, neither laughter nor tears is the desired response, but rather peace which passeth understanding.

The mixture of poetry and prose is matched by a mixture of poetic styles and meters within the verses of the play. E. Martin Browne [in "the Dramatic Verse of T. S. Eliot"] has pointed out that an appropriate style was worked out for each kind of scene:

> The most superficial level, that of the quarrels between Becket and the Knights, is rhymed doggerel. . . . More subtle, and sometimes rather crabbed, is a four-stress rhyming verse for the Tempters who dramatise the tortuous progress of Becket's inner struggle. . . . There is an easy, near-blank-verse for dialogue with the Priests and Women. . . . And for the Chorus, a very varied series of forms, from the three-stress lines of the women's domestic talk . . . to the long complexes of pleading or of praise. . . . In addition, Eliot has followed the precedent he established with his final Chorus in *The Rock* which is based on the Gloria of the Mass and used the rhythms of two more Christian hymns [Dies Irae and Te Deum] as ground-bass of choral order.

Eliot's own account of his verse in *Murder in the Cathedral* is found in "Poetry and Drama" (1951). Since he had to take his audience back to an historical event, he felt that "the vocabulary and style could not be exactly those of modern conversation—as in some modern French plays using the plot and personages of Greek drama." On the other hand, he wished to avoid archaic vocabulary and style because he "wanted to bring home to the audience the contemporary relevance of the situation. The style therefore had to be neutral, committed neither to the present nor to the past." He was aware that it was essential to avoid the Shakespearean echo of blank verse "which, after extensive use for nondramatic poetry, had lost the flexibility which blank verse must have if it is to give the effect of conversation." Because he felt that the rhythm of blank verse had become too remote from the movement of modern speech, he chose as his model the versification of *Everyman*. "An avoidance of too much iambic, some use of alliteration, and occasional unexpected rhyme, helped to distinguish the versification from that of the nineteenth century." He came to feel later that from his point of view *Murder in the Cathedral* was "a dead end" because it did not solve the problem of language for future plays. The versification had only the negative merit of avoiding what had to be avoided; it did not solve the problems of idiom or of metrics for later dramas.

On the surface level which has been described, *Murder in the Cathedral* is a stylized dramatization of the historical situation of the martyrdom of Thomas Becket presented both as a psychological study of the saint and at the same time as a portrayal of the twelfth-century power struggle of church and state made applicable to the modern world.

But, in addition to the surface level, there is another level of meaning beneath the surface which shows the play to be a development of the dramatic theory evolved earlier and exemplified by *Sweeney Agonistes*. Eliot's treatment of the second level of meaning in *Murder in the Cathedral*, however, introduces an important modification of his use of Cornford's ritual scheme in the earlier play. Eliot kept the basic formulations of the Ur-drama but he cast the murdered god in the role of Christ and developed the ritual sequence of events to conform to the Christian interpretation of that pattern in the biblical lore surrounding Christ's Crucifixion and Resurrection.

The playwright integrates this underlying level of meaning with the surface events by constructing an elaborate dramatic analogy between the martyr and Christ, both of whom are portrayed as divine and sin-laden scapegoats who are mutilated and brought back to renewed life. While the martyr as the type of Christ and the presence of elements from the ritual drama have been noted, I believe that neither the completeness of the analogy nor the connection between the theme and the ritual plot has been fully recognized.

Thomas, himself, makes clear the analogy between the martyr and Christ in his Christmas sermon:

I wish only that you should ponder and meditate the deep meaning and mystery of our masses of Christmas Day. For whenever Mass is said, we re-enact the Passion and Death of Our Lord; and on this Christmas Day we do this in celebration of His Birth. So that at the same moment we rejoice in His coming for the salvation of men, and offer again to God His Body and Blood in sacrifice, oblation and satisfaction for the sins of the whole world. . . .

Not only do we at the feast of Christmas celebrate at once Our Lord's Birth and His Death: but on the next day we celebrate the martyrdom of His first martyr, the blessed Stephen. Is it an accident, do you think, that the day of the first martyr follows immediately the day of the Birth of Christ? By no means. Just as we rejoice and mourn at once, in the Birth and in the Passion of Our Lord; so also, in a smaller figure, we both rejoice and mourn in the death of martyrs. We mourn, for the sins of the world that has martyred them; we rejoice, that another soul is numbered among the Saints in Heaven, for the glory of God and for the salvation of men.

The first part of the play, in which Thomas is visited by the Tempters, may thus be viewed as symbolic of Christ's Temptation and the second part, in which Thomas's martyrdom is enacted, as the Passion, Death, and Resurrection of Christ. The opening chorus establishes the analogy between the women drawn to the Cathedral at the Christmas season because of their presentiment of a tremendous event to be enacted and the birth of Christ, in such lines as: "The New Year waits, destiny waits for the coming," and "Shall the Son of Man be born again in the litter of scorn?" The imagery used by the women to express their fear of the coming of life is similar to that used in the opening of *The Waste Land.*

The Herald's description of the coming of the Archbishop into the city echoes Christ's triumphal entry into Jerusalem, even to the colt mentioned in Matthew and Luke and the strewing of garments and branches in Matthew; at the same time it develops the analogy to the procession of Phales mentioned by Cornford and Murray.

Thomas's four temptations, though not exactly analogous to Christ's in the desert, are close enough to be convincing if one equates the Devil's request that Christ turn the stones into bread with the First

Tempter's appeal to Thomas's appetites, the Devil's offer of the kingdoms of the world with the inducements of the Second and Third
Tempters, and the Devil's attempt to make Christ throw himself
down from the pinnacle in order to prove his divinity with the Fourth
Tempter's appeal to Thomas's pride in willing martyrdom. In addition, just as Christ's Sermon on the Mount follows immediately
Christ's temptation in Matthew, so the Christmas sermon of Thomas
follows *his* temptation.

Part 2 contains the agon of the drama, the struggle of the sin-laden
god-figure, in the person of the Archbishop, with his antagonists. It
develops, at the same time, several similarities between the Gospel
accounts of Christ's passion and Thomas's martyrdom. The most obvious analogy is between the Crucifixion of Christ and the murder of
Thomas by the jealous seekers after power in this world, and the acceptance of death by both Christ and the martyr as a part of God's
design for the redemption of mankind. But other similarities also exist:
for example, the supper the Priests mention in the beginning of part 2
may be meant to represent both the Last Supper and the ritual feast,
and the Knights' false accusations against Thomas may be intended to
suggest both the trial of Christ and the battle of insults engaged in by
the god and his antagonist.

Thomas's triumphant statement, just before his death, on the
purification of blood,

> I am a priest,
> A Christian, saved by the blood of Christ,
> Ready to suffer with my blood.
> This is the sign of the Church always,
> The sign of blood. Blood for blood.
> His blood given to buy my life,
> My blood given to pay for His death,
> My death for His death,

emphasizes the reciprocity between Christ's and the martyr's death.
Christ shed his blood for the remission of human sin and the martyr, in
return, sheds his blood both in repayment for and in reenactment of
Christ's sacrifice. Blood is a multiple symbol in the play and the
women view it differently. To them it is symbolic of their blood-guilt
in the shedding of the saint's, and by analogy Christ's, blood:

> The land is foul, the water is foul, our beasts and ourselves
>   defiled with blood.

> A rain of blood has blinded my eyes. Where is England?
>   where is Kent? where is Canterbury?
> O far far far far in the past; and I wander in a land of barren
>   boughs: if I break them, they bleed; I wander in a land
>   of dry stones: if I touch them they bleed.

The theme of blood-guilt is also present in Matthew's version of Pilate's offer to give Christ to the multitude:

> He [Pilate] took water, and washed his hands before the multitude, saying, I am innocent of the blood of this just person: see ye to it. Then answered all the people, and said, His blood be on us, and on our children.

The rain of blood and other lines in the same chorus, including "Night stay with us, stop sun, hold season, let the day not come, let the spring not come," suggest the darkness and earthquake which occurred at Christ's death. The references in the women's chorus to the stones leading to Dante's river of Blood and to the bleeding boughs of the Suicides in the *Inferno* indicate that though the women do not yet realize it, the blood they interpret only as a sign of their terrible guilt will bring them to a penitential state of grace. Thus the death of the martyr and of Christ includes both good and evil, guilt and glory, just as the killing of the god represents both sin and necessity to primitive worshippers.

The concluding lines of the play emphasize a final correspondence between the Savior and the saint. The women, acknowledging their sin, chant:

> Lord, have mercy upon us.
> Christ, have mercy upon us.
> Lord, have mercy upon us.
> Blessed Thomas, pray for us.

The Resurrection of Christ is paralleled by the entrance of Thomas into the ranks of sainthood, and thus the women can pray to both Christ and Thomas for mercy and intercession.

In my opinion *Murder in the Cathedral* is Eliot's most successful integration of his dramatic theories. The levels of the play are intrinsically unified by the skillful interweaving of Thomas's story with the imagery of Christ's Temptation and Passion and with the prototype formula of all religion and drama. The hierarchy of characters within the play who perceive the meaning of Thomas's death on their various levels helps to tighten the unity of the drama and to give it the stylized quality Eliot admires. His chorus, occupying a place midway between the chorus in *Sweeney Agonistes,* which is "material, literal-minded and visionless," and the chorus in *The Rock,* which speaks for the church in action, is by far the most successful of the three. By demonstrating the changing attitude of the chorus in *Murder in the Cathedral* from a fear of spiritual realities and a disavowal of responsibilities to acceptance of and participation in both the sin and glory of martyrdom, Eliot has provided a highly effective vehicle for commentary on the action and participation in it.

Most important of all for the play's effectiveness is the new and less literal conception of rhythm which Eliot used. In *Sweeney Agonistes* the "rhythm" was limited to the syncopation of the jazz meter, whereas in *Murder in the Cathedral* the whole structure becomes rhythmic in the sense that the musical form which Eliot has so often mentioned is achieved. The structural rhythm is achieved by the stylized progression of the action with its undergirding analogies to Christ's life. Part 1, presenting the temptation of Thomas, his lowest ebb, and part 2, presenting his passion, death, and victory, his highest point, provide a kind of circular movement which carries out the wheel imagery. The sermon which divides the two parts is contrasted with the Knights' speeches which are intended to lift the audience from their complacency outside the action to an admission of their own communal guilt, as the chorus has been lifted within the play. The alternation of the events of Thomas's martyrdom with the lyrical reaction of the women is a successful use of the same device which had failed in *The Rock.* For once Eliot's distaste for realism seems to have led to the achievement of the kind of ordered whole and aesthetically satisfying surface which his theory demanded.

The playwright, however, feeling that he had been led away from his goal of creating a drama of contemporary relevance, returned in his next play to the idea behind *Sweeney Agonistes,* the portrayal of the Orestes myth in a modern setting. Despite the surface differences between *Sweeney Agonistes* and *The Family Reunion,* the similarities of method and theme show the latter to be a reworking of the material of the earlier unfinished play. *The Family Reunion* thus marks Eliot's return to a religious drama in which he hoped to show the contemporary world the image of its own spiritual needs by means of a dramatic method already developed and refined in his earlier plays.

Eliot and the Living Theatre

Katharine Worth

No playwright of our time has been more difficult to "see" than Eliot. The poetry and the piety have worked a potent spell, obscuring both dramatic weaknesses and actual or potential strengths. The argument of this essay is that to be seen in perspective Eliot's plays must be seen in the context of the living theatre, not as an extension of the poetry and the dramatic theory, nor as a special kind of activity called "religious drama."

We know that Eliot desperately wanted to elude the kind of audiences who attended his early plays expecting "to be patiently bored and to satisfy themselves with the feeling that they have done something meritorious." His anxiety to make contact with "real" audiences was an important factor in the evolution of his postwar style. He put the poetry on a thin diet and overlaid his symbols with a conventionally seductive facade.

Yet the plays seem to keep their place in the not very jolly corner labelled "verse and religious drama." Is the reason for this simply their inadequacy as plays? Must they always be performed in what Ivor Brown jocularly called "the crypt of St. Eliot's" and have they no relevance to the development of the modern theatre? Are they quite out of the main stream, as far out as the plays of Masefield, Drinkwater and Stephen Phillips are now seen to have been?

I do not believe that we have to answer "yes" to these questions, though much of the existing criticism of the drama, no doubt against

From *Eliot in Perspective: A Symposium,* edited by Graham Martin. © 1970 by Macmillan Press Ltd.

its intention, forces us to do so by emphasising so heavily moral patterns, Christian solutions and thematic progressions. What in my view emerges as theatrically interesting, and what gives Eliot a place, however tentative, in the mainstream, is his feeling for alienation and violence, his gift for suggesting metaphysical possibilities in the trivial or absurd and his exploration of new dramatic means for working upon the nerves and pulses of an audience.

Of course these potentialities are imperfectly realised. Again and again he seems to be on the verge of striking out an entirely new line, of creating, even, the modern theatre. Then he abandons the promising experiment, conceals the real experience. *Sweeney Agonistes* must be one of the most exciting beginnings ever made by a poet turning towards the theatre, a Yeatsian concept of total theatre, full of primitive power. *The Family Reunion* showed that the impulse of the fragments could be sustained in a full-length piece and opened out still new vistas; even in *The Cocktail Party,* though not acknowledged for what it is, sounds the note of Beckett and Pinter; not irrelevantly, as M. C. Bradbrook has noted, do the title and situation of the play bring into mind *The Birthday Party.*

What these experiments grew from, why they were not followed up and Eliot's dramatic powers fully realised, are the questions we might expect criticism to be asking. But, on the contrary, critics tend to accept the idea of painful self-improvement from *The Rock* to *The Cocktail Party* which Eliot offers in "Poetry and Drama." Few would be found, of course, to place the last plays, *The Confidential Clerk* and *The Elder Statesman,* at the summit of his achievement. These are fairly generally admitted to show a falling away of power, though even here, to some minds, the edification in the subject matter is more than compensation for thinness of texture. And there will, no doubt, always be some for whom *Murder in the Cathedral* has no need to abide our questions: "Of the greatness of *Murder in the Cathedral,* there can be no doubt—it may even be the greatest religious play ever written—and the other plays will survive if only as parts of the unity of which it is the finest element" (D. E. Jones, *The Plays of T. S. Eliot*). But setting aside these acts of homage to the subject-matter, it has still been common form for Eliot's own chart of his progress to be taken as a basis for study, for *The Cocktail Party* to be seen, as he presents it, as a dramatic advance upon *The Family Reunion,* and for *Sweeney Agonistes* to be totally ignored.

Eliot is, then, not without responsibility for a situation in which his real theatrical powers are not recognised. In small ways, too, he has encouraged an untheatrical view, by allowing recordings of the choruses detached from their dramatic context; indeed, by making them himself, in a voice admirably suited to *Four Quartets* but hardly likely to increase our belief in the real existence of the Women of Canterbury. The early publication of *Sweeney Agonistes* in *Collected Poems* (1936) and its subsequent omission from *Collected Plays* (1962) has also served to misdirect. Even critics such as Northrop Frye and G. S. Fraser here referred to this most exciting theatrical piece as a "poem."

Criticism of poetic drama in our time has often taken untheatrical directions for want of a theatrical context, but there is no need for this in Eliot's case. A wealth of theatrical material exists, from reviews and actors' accounts of their roles to records of the growth of the texts under the pressure of stage requirements.

Two kinds of interest attach to this material. It has, in the first place, the interest which firsthand accounts of plays in preparation and production must always have for students of drama, offering a perspective which can never be quite the same as that from the study. In the second place, it raises questions about Eliot's special kind of relationship with the theatre world. Some of those involved in production of his plays were deeply committed to the idea of a "religious drama"; their commentaries often combine shrewd stage judgements with a tendency, common in nontheatrical criticism, to look through what is there in the play to what ought to be there.

How important was the influence from within the theatrical milieu in turning Eliot towards the morality patterns of the late plays is, indeed, one of the as yet unanswerable questions with which future criticism must be concerned. It is already clear from E. Martin Browne's illuminating accounts of his share in the plays (especially from *The Making of a Play* [1966]) that his own influence was of the greatest importance. In giving Eliot much needed advice on stage necessity, he was also moving him towards a less ambiguous and equivocal expression of theme; suggesting such changes as the replacement of the word "daimon," by "guardian" in Edward's analysis of his own condition and requiring an exact account of Celia's fate, which Eliot, we are told, had in the first draft left "as vague as, at the end of *The Family Reunion,* he had at first left Harry's." Whether this last change really was an improvement is a question to which different answers have been and will be given, according to whether the play is seen as the Christian morality it purports to be, or as an abortive attempt at a less easily defined structure, in which the word "daimon" is in fact the right one.

The many critics, in and out of the theatre, who are in sympathy with Eliot's doctrinal intentions, will hardly recognise the existence of such alternatives, or will at least have no hesitation in emphasising the orthodox interpretation of any play under discussion. But even the criticism uncommitted to a religious viewpoint sometimes seems slightly out of focus with what is happening in the plays, perhaps because critical argument is so often conducted in a context composed almost exclusively of Eliot's own theory and practice. Much light has been thrown on the plays by studies of the relation of theory and practice and of the plays to the poems, of sources and meaning, ritual and symbolic patterns. Yet the separation of the play from the theatrical context has its dangers, not least the danger of over-interpretation. A critic, like C. H. Smith, who tells us [in *Eliot's Dramatic Theory*] that she is "not primarily concerned with an evaluation of Eliot's work by current theatrical standards" may have, and, indeed, has many valuable insights to offer about the ritualistic overtones, but she is also liable to move a long way from stage or any other kind of reality, as she does in her account of Harcourt Reilly: "Sir Henry's ritual identity is suggested by his continual drink of gin with a drop of water (he is adulterating his spiritual nature with a drop of water, representing time, flux, and humanity)."

Religious influences may have been reinforced by the didactic drama of Auden and Isherwood, who, perhaps inspired by the printed version of *Sweeney Agonistes,* were pursuing the direction indicated in it during the years when *The Rock, Murder in the Cathedral* and *The Family Reunion* were being written. The Group Theatre who produced their plays were dedicated to the exploration of popular techniques; they envisaged a new drama, "analogous to modern musical comedy or the pre-medieval folk play," and in pursuit of this curious-sounding goal they explored the possibilities in dance, jazz effects and visual shock tactics such as masks.

"We should like less prancing and bad dancing" was Geoffrey Grigson's comment on the Group Theatre style, a remark which perhaps Eliot might have endorsed if, as Professor Isaacs tells us [in *An Assessment of Twentieth-Century Literature*] he was "puzzled" by the production the theatre gave *Sweeney Agonistes* in 1935. He may well have considered that the notion of putting his characters into full or half masks destroyed the delicate tension he had built up between a commonplace surface and a profoundly disturbing under-pattern. Yet, in giving him a production of his play, and in drawing his attention to Auden and Isherwood in performance, the Group Theatre were encouraging him to continue his exploration of the possibilities in revue techniques. Certainly, *Murder in the Cathedral* owes a good deal of its theatrical life to flamboyant changes of rhythm. Its contemporary political flavour, too, in the totalitarian apologetics of the Knights, seems to point to the engaged drama of Auden and Isherwood, as later *The Family Reunion* was to show some striking similarities to *The Ascent of F6.*

If there was then this influence operating in *Murder in the Cathedral,* it is not likely to have lessened Eliot's difficulties in dealing with ordinary people like the Women of Canterbury and showing them in a convincing human relationship with Becket, or, indeed, with anyone else in the play. The characteristic hero of Auden and Isherwood, in all his high-minded liberalism, has as little real contact with the "people" whose cause he espouses as has Ransom of *The Ascent of F6* with the suburban Mr and Mrs A, isolated in their stage boxes.

The isolation in that instance is deliberate. But in *Murder in the Cathedral* the isolated elements are meant to coalesce, Chorus and Saint to come together in the redemption of one by the death of the other. That there has been an interior happening of this kind is declared poetically with such skill as almost to convince that it has happened dramatically too. But it has not. The Chorus are not involved in any human relationship with Becket real enough to move belief in his having power to affect their lives. They are only a collective voice, not living people with a stake in the action. Becket addresses them, typically from a physical height above them, in the pulpit, but hardly speaks to them. Whether his awareness of them affects his own inner development is extremely debatable. Production could certainly make it seem that when he has his moment of illumination—

> Now is my way clear, now is the meaning plain:
> Temptation shall not come in this kind again—

it comes to him through listening to the entreaties of the Chorus,

> O Thomas Archbishop, save us, save us, save yourself that
> we may be saved;
> Destroy yourself and we are destroyed.

But the recognition could with equal, if not greater theatrical plausibility, be shown as self-generated, coming out of the deep trance of self-communion in which Becket is engaged for most of the play.

Eliot admitted to having difficulty in imagining the chorus; it seems that he was able to imagine their thoughts, but not what they were actually doing, particularly at the crisis of the murder. If they are present at this event, it can only be as mute spectators, like the Priests who, as the director of the film version, George Hoellering, pointed out, "do not lift a finger to come to his aid." No attempt is made to express their helplessness as a dramatic element, nor is any notice taken of Chorus and Priests by the Knights, who, after the murder, address the audience directly, giving them the orders which, if given to the Chorus would have helped to involve them as human beings in the situation: "I suggest that you now disperse quietly to your homes. Please be careful not to loiter in groups at street corners, and do nothing that might provoke any public outbreak."

The various changes made in the film version were in the first place a response to the demands of the different medium; the Knights could not address a cinema audience at such length, so they had to be shown speaking to a crowd outside the cathedral. But some of these changes would, as Hoellering suggested, improve stage versions too; he saw the need for "tightening" the action by integrating the Women of Canterbury more closely into it and for increasing credibility by some quite simple rearrangements such as the dismissal of the Priests to vespers before the murder. Eliot accepted these alterations as "improvements" in a statement of some ambiguity: the play worked in the Chapter House at Canterbury, he implies, because it was not really trying to be a play there: the film version "made the meaning clearer, and in that way is nearer to what the play would have been, had it been written for the London theatre and by a dramatist of greater experience."

In failing to come to life as a play about the interaction of people, *Murder in the Cathedral* fails to become the new kind of play Eliot's religious belief compelled him to attempt. It is weakest in those areas where themes of Christian redemption and brotherhood are being worked out, as the precarious attachment of the Chorus to the action shows. Where it has strength is in precisely that territory already shown in *Sweeney Agonistes* to be Eliot's own. The central action is, indeed, curiously close to the action outlined in the earlier play. Eliot himself points to its extreme simplicity: "A man comes home, foreseeing that he will be killed, and he is killed." Anticipation of, and preparation for, an act of violence generates the greatest dramatic excitement felt anywhere in the piece. Becket is most fully realised as a human character when he is involved with the idea of death, in the preparatory clearing of conscience with the Four Tempters and in the murder scene itself, where the intimacy of his relationship with his murderers, usually stressed in production by the doubling of Tempters' and Knights' roles, goes far beyond the degree of intimacy he achieves with anyone else in the play.

The Chorus, too, finds the most dramatic of all its functions in winding up the suspense as the murder approaches, then releasing it in a great outburst which in its exultingly violent rhythms, conveys a Maenad-like impression of ecstasy in the sacrificial consummation:

> Clear the air! clean the sky! wash the wind! take the stone
>   from the stone . . . Wash the stone, wash the bone . . .
>   wash them wash them!

They may not be able to communicate as personalities, but they do, though with some monotony, convey a state of mind with which Eliot is, dramatically speaking, at home; a state of "panic and emptiness." "The sense of disgust in the chorus," says Stevie Smith [in "History or Poetic Drama?"] "is the most living thing out of all the play." The word "living" is correct here; their "disgust" grows out of the action, moves with it and is finally appeased in the ritual killing.

Fascination with violence as a cleansing, therapeutic process is strongly felt in *Murder in the Cathedral.* Virginia Woolf once said, "If you are anaemic as Tom is, there is a glory in blood"; without accepting her explanation of the cause, we may agree with her findings. There is a kind of glory in blood and violence in the plays, violence as a means of opening the doors of perception.

Fear in the Way:
The Design of Eliot's Drama

Michael Goldman

We know and do not know what it is to act and suffer. How do we come to know more? The answer, given in every play, is: *watch and wait*. But watching and waiting imply a crucial dramatic problem, and the success or failure of each of Eliot's plays may be said to hinge on its solution. At some point in the drawing-room plays, the dramatic convention becomes a fragmented background against which certain characters are seen in a new light, isolated in a freshly haunted world. But this means that there is a risk that the continuity of the action may evaporate, sustained as it has been by the apparent connectedness of the play's world and the now-discredited significance of the ghosts haunting it. At the same time there is the danger that the dramatic interest of the central character may evaporate too. The watching and waiting theme requires that at some moment the hero surrender his role as an agent; he must consent to be passive. He is displaced from a central initiating role to become part of the pattern. The moment of surrender may itself make for a good scene: as when Edward accepts his becoming a thing, an object in the hands of masked actors, or Mulhammer gives up control to Eggerson and Guzzard and absorbs the bewildering results. Claverton struggles with a version of this necessity in his first long speech and again accepts it in the strong scene at the end of his play, and Thomas's surrender is perhaps most powerfully felt in his long cry at the moment of death, which Eliot has considerably expanded from the historical records. But essentially what a

From *Eliot in His Time,* edited by A. Walton Litz. ©1973 by Princeton University Press.

character accepts at a moment like this is that he must no longer be a *performer*—and this has awkward implications, both for actor and playwright.

Watching and waiting over any period of time is not very dramatic; it is always a problem for an actor, and Eliot cannot be said always to have solved it. At the very end of *The Elder Statesman,* Claverton says, "In becoming no one, I begin to live," but the actor of this often ungrateful role might fairly complain that, instead of becoming no one, the play limits him to *being* no one for most of its length, that he must watch and wait from the beginning. And in *The Family Reunion,* once the interest of the false ghosts peters out and there is no crime to be uncovered, Eliot can devise no action that engages any of the characters; we are treated to a series of explanations that never become encounters. From *The Cocktail Party* on, Eliot is always able to maintain action and encounter, because the haunting function, both false and true, is taken over by real characters who can make their presence felt in a lively way whenever they appear. Reilly, Julia, Guzzard, Carghill, Gomez—these are good parts, not hard to act. But for the last two plays there remains a difficulty in casting the leading roles which makes it problematical whether *The Confidential Clerk* and *The Elder Statesman* will ever receive performances that can test their best values. In many ways they ask more of their actors than they offer in return. Claverton must be played by an actor not only strong but abnormally unselfish, ready to pass honestly through the long passivity of the early acts in order to contribute to the lovely finale. In *The Confidential Clerk* the problem is even more serious. The characterization of Sir Claude as a financier is extremely flimsy, and his lack of definition as a public figure makes the first act dangerously slack. The deep problem, however, is Colby, whose interest lies far too much in the eyes of his beholders. He must be cast against his part; the role must be filled by an immensely engaging, physically robust actor with no suggestion of priggishness or passivity about him. Here, clearly, the production must make up for weaknesses in the text. Whether we shall ever get such a production, however, remains to be seen.

So far I have been talking mostly about the plays written after *Murder in the Cathedral,* since the subject of ghosts has a special bearing on Eliot's treatment of the drawing-room convention. But my remarks apply to the earlier play as well, for the pattern I have described helps to account for *Murder in the Cathedral*'s dramatic effectiveness and points to meanings that have been overlooked in criticism and production. Let me begin with an objection that is frequently raised against the play: "The determining flaw in *Murder in the Cathedral* is that the imitation of its action is complete at the end of Part One." I do not think this is true to our felt experience of the play, even in a good amateur production, nor to the dramatic intentions clearly indicated in the text.

It is true that by the end of part 1 we have seen Thomas accept his martyrdom as part of a pattern to which he must consent for the right reasons, and that we see this acceptance reenacted both in the sermon and in part 2, with no modification of theme or deepening of Thomas's response. But the point of the play lies in the reenactment, since everything is changed *for us* by each reseeing. The aim of *Murder in the Cathedral* is to make its audience "watch and wait," to "bear witness"—to see the event in several perspectives, each enriching the other, so the pattern may subsist, so the action may be seen as pattern, and so that our own relation to the action, our part of the pattern, may be fully and intensely experienced—and this is not finally accomplished until the very end of the play.

Once more it is a question of knowing and not knowing. Even as the play begins, we know what its climax will be. But by the time we actually see Thomas murdered, after witnessing part 1 and the sermon, we see that we knew and did not know. In the same way, the Knights and the Chorus, lacking the knowledge we have, both know and do not know what they are doing and suffering. And of course after the murder, the Knights' speeches show us yet one more aspect of the event that we knew and did not know.

It should be noted at this point that bearing witness, watching the events of the play, is from the first associated both with knowing and not knowing and with fear. In performance we are apt to be unaware of the powerful theatricality of the opening chorus. The theatrical problems of the Women of Canterbury are generally approached by way of voice production and enunciation, and we are grateful—and lucky—if the actresses recruited for the occasion manage to speak clearly and on the beat. Choral acting, as opposed to choral reciting, is usually beyond them. But Eliot understands, as no one except Lorca since the Greeks has understood, that choral writing is writing for the body, and the bodily excitement of the first Chorus derives from the way it joins the feeling of knowing and not knowing to the emotion of fear. The Chorus prefigures the action to come and combines it with a bewildered self-consciousness. We move, they say. We wait. Why do we move and wait as we do? Is it fear, is it the allure of safety, is it even the allure of fear? What kind of fear, what kind of safety? This is exactly the question the play will put about martyrdom, put to Thomas and to us:

> Here let us stand, close by the cathedral. Here let us wait.
> Are we drawn by danger? Is it the knowledge of safety, that
>   draws our feet
> Towards the cathedral? What danger can be
> For us, the poor, the poor women of Canterbury? what
>   tribulation
> With which we are not already familiar? There is no danger
> For us, and there is no safety in the cathedral. Some presage
>   of an act
> Which our eyes are compelled to witness, has forced our feet
> Towards the cathedral. We are forced to bear witness.

The opportunity for the actors is remarkable. The tension between fear and freedom on which the chorus is grounded might fairly be called the root emotion of the theater; it is the same emotion, for instance, that a shaman and his audience share when he begins to impersonate the spirits that are haunting him. The emotion here is intensified through group response, beautifully registered in the language, and profoundly integrated with the action of the play. A crowd of women huddles toward the protection of what it half senses to be a fearful place. The chorus rouses the audience toward the awareness to come, of the church and martyrdom as a painful and difficult shelter.

Thomas is an easier dramatic subject for Eliot than his later heroes, because he remains active all the time he is on stage, aggressive even while he waits and watches. He is supremely connected to this world and the next, secure in his being except for the crisis at the climax of part 1. As far as it bears on Thomas, the pattern of haunting is complete when he says, "Now is my way clear." The true nature of the shadows he must strive with has been revealed to him and he is no longer isolated. We have seen [elsewhere] however, that in the later dramas the pattern of haunting continues to the end of the play and works itself out in the lives of characters for whom such transcendence is not possible. I would like to urge that this pattern is also present in *Murder in the Cathedral*. The sustained pattern of haunting completes the play's design after Thomas's death, and by means of a carefully prepared shift of focus imparts to the whole drama a final richness of impression too easily neglected both in the study and on the stage. As the play finds its structure in our bearing witness to Thomas's martyrdom and, through the Chorus, associates our watching and waiting with a fear that is at times close to panic, so the haunting in the play, the fear in the way of the original title, is finally brought to bear not on Thomas but on the Chorus and on us.

The sequence of events that concludes the play, beginning with the moment the Knights attack Thomas in the cathedral, testifies to Eliot's remarkable control over the resources of his stage. Thomas cries out at length, and the murder continues throughout the entire chorus which begins, "Clear the air! clean the sky!" The stage directions make quite certain of this. The drunken Knights, then, take upwards of three minutes—a very long time on the stage—to hack Thomas to death, while the Chorus chants in terror. Beyond the insistent horror of the act itself there is a further effect of juxtaposition achieved between the murder and the action of the Chorus. Properly acted, the choral text unavoidably suggests that in its terror the Chorus is somehow egging the murderers on, that the continuing blows of the Knights are accomplishing what the violent, physical, heavily accented cries for purgation call for: "Clear the air! clean the sky! wash the wind! take the stone from the stone, take the skin from the arm, take the muscle from the bone, and wash them. Wash the stone, wash the bone, wash the brain, wash the soul, wash them wash them!" The Chorus brings to a flooding climax the ambivalent current of fear that has haunted the Women of Canterbury from the opening scene—attraction toward Thomas and a powerful aversion from him, fear for and of the martyr. The murder is felt not only as a protracted physical horror but as an action in which the Chorus has participated.

The speeches of the Knights that follow are of course sinister as well as comic. The two effects are connected, as Eliot seems well aware, for our laughter involves us, as their fear has involved the Chorus, in aggression toward Thomas. We laugh with release from the constraints of fancy-dress. In the style they adopt, the Knights voice our own impulse to deflate the bubble of archaism, poetry, and saintliness. We share their animus, and their arguments turn the point against us. They have acted in our interests, as de Morville reminds us. "If there is any guilt whatever in the matter you must share it with us."

It is not the confident Third Priest with his dismissal of the Knights as weak, sad men, who has the last word, but the Women of Canterbury, who acknowledge themselves as types of the common man, weak and sad indeed. At the end they dwell upon their fear, which is no less strong for the transcendence they have witnessed. As in all Eliot's plays, the glimpse of transcendence is in itself a source of fear for those who have been left behind. They make the point the Knights have made in argument and that the choral accompaniment of the murder has powerfully enforced:

> That the sin of the world is upon our heads; that the blood of
> the martyrs and the agony of the saints
> Is upon our heads.

I would suggest that everything that happens in the play from the moment the Knights raise their swords has been designed to give these lines a weight of conviction and a dramatic force that I hope I may by now characterize with some precision—as haunting.

The treatment of the Chorus, then, establishes the pattern Eliot was to maintain in his later drama. And the pattern in turn reflects the originality and strength of his writing for the theater. What Eliot discovered was a way to make drama out of the central subject of his poetry and criticism—the calamitous loss of self and imprisonment in self that haunts our era, a disease that may drive the fortunate man to glimpse transcendence, but which even those glimpses cannot cure:

> The enduring is not a substitute for the transient
> Neither one for the other.
>
> ("A Note on War Poetry")

The theme pursues Eliot in all his work. In drama, his success was to make the sense of pursuit a ground for action and the theme a source of design, to transmit to his audiences the haunting pressure of "the enduring" on those who, like us, are condemned to roles as actors in a transient world.

Murder in the Cathedral:
The Pain of Purgatory

David Ward

The Rock is a failure, an uneasy association of modes in which a crude expressionism alternates with rather flaccid experiments in the choric mode. Eliot's ear for the rhythms and intonations of British working class speech which had served him well in *The Waste Land II* fails him: the language of the workmen in *The Rock* is self-conscious parody, and though Eliot's intention is far more sympathetic to his subjects than it is in "A Game of Chess," the final result is a far more contemptuous debasement of the dialect than in *The Waste Land,* where the cockney speech at least has a kind of vigorous flatness and sloppiness.

As E. Martin Browne has made clear, the difficulties in producing a pageant of this kind were immense. The mixture of modes did not escape attention at the time of production. *The Times* review, quoted by Browne, begins "The theatre, that long-lost child of the English Church, made a notable reunion with its parent last night. Mr Eliot's pageant play looked first to liturgy for its dramatic form, though wisely imitating also the ready and popular stage modes, such as music-hall, ballet and mime." The combination of modes in *Murder in the Cathedral* is far more integral to the purpose and the sentiment, and though it must always remain a rather special case in the drama, the play is an astonishing success. In "Poetry and Drama" Eliot speaks of the audience which crowds into religious festivals, expecting to be "patiently bored and to satisfy themselves with the feeling that they have done

From *T. S. Eliot: Between Two Worlds.* © 1973 by David Ward. Routledge & Kegan Paul, 1973.

something meritorious." *Murder in the Cathedral* is a special case partly because Eliot does not accept the easy way out offered by such a complaisant audience, and faces the problems of religious drama with courage and intelligence; but also because Eliot is sympathetically aware of the needs and problems of his audience, and this forces a greater directness and paradoxically, despite the special limitations of the spectators, a greater universality. While it is true, as Eliot said in his essay on "Marie Lloyd," that the artist needs "the collaboration of the audience with the artist," it is equally true that the audience needs an artist who is temperamentally capable of collaborating with *them,* and in these special circumstances Eliot discovers the skill. He declared in 1934: "With the disappearance of the idea of intense moral struggle, the human beings presented to us both in poetry and prose fiction today...tend to become less real. It is in fact during moments of moral and spiritual struggle...that men and women come nearest being real" (*After Strange Gods*). In any usual sense of the word both *Sweeney Agonistes* and *Murder in the Cathedral* are far from "realistic," but (whether or not *Sweeney* would have achieved it) it is this special kind of realism which both were aiming at. However, the struggle or conflict is not expressed simply in terms of a character study. The drama is focused upon Thomas and in one sense the conflict is within him; in another sense it is in all the characters as they participate in the action; in another sense it is intended to be in the audience in so far as they are drawn into the play to participate in the drama themselves. Thus we must be aware as we experience the drama that, just as all the men and women of *The Waste Land* meet in Tiresias, so all the characters in *Murder in the Cathedral* reflect or represent potential or actual states of Thomas's being—tempters, priests, knights and chorus—and that he in turn is the focus of the drama of the whole community. And Thomas's agon and pathos, his conflict and suffering, are made into a communal experience to be entered into by the modern audience, just as is the apprehension and then the joy of the chorus and the sophistries, the crudenesses and destructiveness of the tempters and the knights:

> But for every evil, every sacrilege,
> Crime, wrong, oppression and the axe's edge,
> Indifference, exploitation, you and you,
> And you, must all be punished. So must you.

The last sentence is spoken directly to the audience. But though Eliot assumes and declares the responsibility of every one of us in a community of guilt: "the sin of the world is upon our heads. . . the blood of the martyrs and the agony of the saints / Is upon our heads," the responsibility has its credit side too—we share in Thomas's guilt but may also share ritually in the triumph of his martyrdom; his death may bring new life to the community of which we are part.

Murder in the Cathedral is the play which most clearly declares its ritual origin: it was designed for performance in a place of worship and Eliot himself has declared that its versification owes something to *Everyman,* a play which has equally clearly departed not very far from the original liturgical impulse. But its formal structure, like that of *Sweeney Agonistes,* seems to be modelled upon an anthropological interpretation of Greek drama. Cornford's *The Origin of Attic Comedy* is an application to Aristophanic comedy of the general line of investigation opened up by Gilbert Murray in his "Excursus on the Ritual Forms Preserved in Greek Tragedy" which was published in 1912 as part of Jane Harrison's *Themis.* Murray conceives of the origin of Greek tragedy as aetiological ritual—the celebration of the supposed historical cause of a current ritual practice. *Murder in the Cathedral* is not precisely an aetiological ritual in this sense, but it does commemorate the historical origin of the shrine of St. Thomas, an object of pilgrimage and of veneration for Christians for many centuries. Murray, like Cornford, argues that whatever particular event is celebrated in Greek drama, and whichever hero is protagonist, the *Sacer Ludus* is essentially and originally in celebration of the death and resurrection of the dying god, most typically in his manifestation as Dionysus. As in his poems Eliot conflates the pagan and the Christian myths, reconstructing and enriching the Christian myth with pagan parallels. Thomas's pathos is, as, in a sense, are the sufferings of all the Christian martyrs, an imitation of Christ. Thomas's agon, his exchanges with the Four Tempters, is partly modelled on the temptation of Christ by Satan in the wilderness. But there is no need to repeat here the ways in which Eliot and the anthropologists who influenced him found parallels between the Crucifixion and the passion of the dying fertility god, between Christ's temptation and the motif of the testing of the hero in ancient myth.

Here, then, is Murray's analysis of the prototypical elements of Greek tragedy, with comments on their adaptation in *Murder in the Cathedral.* Eliot's play begins with a *Prologue* or exposition scene which is present in all Greek tragedies except for *Supplices* and *Persae.* Then, following Murray's pattern, there is "1. An *Agon* or Contest, the Year against its enemy, Light against Darkness, Summer against Winter."

In *Murder in the Cathedral* the antagonist is split into Four Tempters, but as is made clear in many ways, the four are merely different manifestations of one antagonist. After this Eliot has an Interlude, Thomas preaching on Christmas morning. Then follows, as in Murray's analysis: "2. A *Pathos* of the Year-Daimon, generally a ritual or sacrificial death, in which Adonis or Attis is slain by the tabu animal, the Pharmakos stoned, Osiris, Dionysus, Pentheus, Orpheus, Hippolytus torn to pieces"—or, in *Murder in the Cathedral*, Thomas is stabbed to death by the Four Knights. In Greek tragedy the Pathos rarely occurs on the stage, so Murray's next stage is "3. A *Messenger"* announcing the death. Since Eliot acts out the Pathos in the play itself the scene is replaced by the address of the Four Knights, justifying their actions as in a public meeting. Then in Murray's scheme comes: "4. A *Threnos* or Lamentation. Specially characteristic, however, is the clash of contrary emotions, the death of the old being the triumph of the new." This describes precisely the last scene of *Murder in the Cathedral.*

Murray goes on to add sections 5 and 6, the *Anagnorisis* and the *Theophany,* but argues that, in the prototypical tragedy, these elements were reserved for the Satyr play which follows the trilogy, and that when the custom of the Satyr play was discontinued, not all tragedians elected to assimilate these two elements into the tragedy. In *Murder in the Cathedral* Anagnorisis and Theophany are absent, though one might think of Thomas's eventual canonization as being a historical consummation of these elements.

The adoption of Murray's analysis of tragedy has some curious and important results. Since the neoclassical period of criticism the theory of tragedy has commonly been based upon Aristotle's *Poetics.* The range of possible interpretations of Aristotle has been very wide indeed and many, perhaps most, writers of tragedies have used Aristotle second-hand, depending upon critical middlemen or imitating and adapting their contemporaries or predecessors. But certain prescriptions for tragedy have retained their classic status, and many of them are ignored by Eliot in *Murder in the Cathedral* and to a lesser extent in *The Family Reunion.* In Aristotle's scheme "The change of fortune should be not from bad to good, but, reversely, from good to bad. It should come about as the result not of vice but of some great error or frailty." Both Thomas and Harry triumph over error and frailty and move from bad to good. "A perfect tragedy . . . should, moreover, imitate actions which excite pity and fear," "through pity and fear effecting the purgation of these emotions." In *Murder in the Cathedral,* pity and fear are the staple emotions of the Chorus, and are evoked from the audience too, perhaps, but the victory of the hero is so nearly complete that it removes him beyond the reach of pity and fear, making those emotions irrelevant; our pity and fear are transferred from the hero to the Chorus and the Knights. In *The Family Reunion* too, we may feel pity and fear for Harry at the beginning, but the hero goes beyond them, neutralizing both emotions; it is Amy who suffers the fall and excites pity and fear in the audience, but she cannot be considered the hero of the play.

In Aristotle's classification, then, neither *Murder in the Cathedral* nor *The Family Reunion* can be considered a true tragedy. There are very few tragedies which can; Shakespeare's tragedies do not observe the unities of place and time and are very liberal in their interpretation of unity of action, for instance, whereas Eliot is fairly meticulous about all three unities. But the "rules" which Eliot breaks are "rules" which have not often been broken by dramatists working consciously within a tragic tradition (at least since Aristotle, for Greek tragedies themselves very often do not fit the Aristotelian prescriptions). It may be asked how Eliot, the champion of tradition, could ignore such well established conventions. The answer is that he felt that he was observing and respecting the tradition in a much more fundamental way than the neo–Aristotelian, searching for the essence of tragedy in its ritual function and its communal purpose. It follows from this view of tragedy that purgation of pity and fear should be secondary motives; that the principal effect of the tragedy should be participation of the audience into a community which has no use any more for fear and pity. "The Mass is a small drama, having all the unities," but it fails to meet Aristotle's other specifications in much the same way as *Murder in the Cathedral* does.

The dramatis personae of the Mass are the celebrant, the communicant and the congregation as chorus, but the end of the drama is the absorption of each persona into one who is present in all the personae, Christ. And the history of each hero, whether the all–embracing heroic figure of Christ or those who imitate his history, the communicants and the celebrants, is not decline and fall, but a symbolic death and triumphant rebirth. To call the Mass a drama is in a way a piece of coat-trailing, but it does suggest various ways in which the experience of drama and specifically tragedy may parallel the experience of the Mass, and the way in which both experiences might have grown from certain persistent human habits and needs. And the tendency of Murray's argument is to confirm the parallels and to suggest the existence of pre-Christian parallels for Christian rituals in the daimon dance and seasonal myths.

It follows naturally enough from the structural basis suggested by Murray that there should be implicit reference throughout *Murder in the Cathedral* to the symbolism of vegetation ritual. The first chorus, for instance, establishes a seasonal symbolism very clearly:

> Since golden October declined into sombre November
> And the apples were gathered and stored, and the land
>   became brown sharp points of death in a waste of
>   water and mud,
> The New Year waits, breathes, waits, whispers in darkness.

It is the waste land of winter; but, as in *The Waste Land,* the barrenness of winter has at least the comfortableness of something known and the Chorus fear the unexpected which will begin the destructive cycle again: "Now I fear disturbance of the quiet seasons." The extraordinary incident which the Chorus awaits with fear that it will disturb the comfort of barrenness is, in point of time, the new year. In the pagan metaphor this is precisely the time of the agony of the dying god; the winter solstice when the new year struggles with the old. In the Christian metaphor it is the time of Christ's birth, when an old world ends and a new begins. The foreboding of the Chorus anticipates the struggle of Thomas the hero with his king, a death, and a rebirth of the spirit: conflict is sensed as disaster, as something passively to be borne:

>   Some presage of an act
> Which our eyes are compelled to witness, has forced our feet
> Towards the cathedral. We are forced to bear witness.

In the state of consciousness which the Chorus manifests at this point this action, *any* action, must be performed by somebody else. They imagine themselves to be simply spectators of the drama—and in this they represent the audience who watch them. The season of sacrifice has to be renewed by repeated martyrdom, but somebody else's:

> Come, happy December, who shall observe you, who shall
>   preserve you?
> Shall the Son of Man be born again in a litter of scorn?
> For us, the poor, there is no action,
> But only to wait and witness.

However, Eliot is not prepared to allow either Chorus or audience to be entirely spectators; the drama is shaped towards ritual purposes, and ritual inevitably involves participation: it is the way in which the tribe or the community reaffirms and re-creates the consciousness of its identity—and the struggle, the suffering and the triumph of the hero are its own agon, pathos and theophany. The Chorus in its forebodings recognizes this, leading the audience gently into the recognition:

> O Thomas, return, Archbishop; return, return to France.
> Return. Quickly. Quietly. Leave us to perish in quiet.
> You come with applause, you come with rejoicing, but you
>   come bringing death into Canterbury:
> A doom on the house, a doom on yourself, a doom on the
>   world.

Their fears are a kind of response to the speech of the third priest; his speech in its turn is a reconciliation of the blind fears of the first priest and the blind hopes of the second. The third priest employs the wheel symbolism which has become familiar to us in *Ash-Wednesday:* "The wheel has been still, these seven years, and no good. / For ill or good, let the wheel turn. / For who knows the end of good and evil?" As against the Chorus's desire to avoid the drama, the third priest welcomes it, knowing how much good and evil interpenetrate each other, how necessary the process which is feared and desired; how the reconciliation is impossible without the conflict. In another sense the priest is recognizing the *magical* functions of Thomas. The wheel has been still for seven years, the period of Thomas's absence; his return imparts movement to the wheel of change, as the agony and the passion of the dying god in the ancient myths causes the cycle of the seasons to begin anew.

Thomas enters, announcing the paradox of action and suffering which underlies the drama of agon and pathos, and the paradox of the role of the Chorus (and the audience) in the drama, the half perceived necessity of *participation* in his own action and suffering in order that action and suffering may be transcended:

> They know and do not know, what it is to act or suffer.
> They know and do not know, that action is suffering
> And suffering is action. Neither does the agent suffer
> Nor the patient act. But both are fixed

> In an eternal action, an eternal patience
> To which all must consent that it may be willed
> And which all must suffer that they may will it,
> That the pattern may subsist, for the pattern is the action
> And the suffering, that the wheel may turn and still
> Be forever still.

In one sense, Thomas is an agent; his return sets the wheel in motion again. In one sense he is a patient; he suffers himself to be killed. But in another sense he is neither, since neither his action nor his suffering proceed from his own personal will; they proceed from the pattern of God's design. A similar distinction is made in Richard Hooker's *The Laws of Ecclesiastical Polity,* between "natural agent" and "voluntary agent." Man possesses free will, but his ability to act voluntarily is given him so that he can obey the natural law, that eternal order which Thomas calls "the pattern" which is at once "an eternal action" and "an eternal patience." The moral struggle, then, which takes place in the agon, is between Thomas and his personal will, and Thomas's triumph is the destruction of his will so that he becomes neither agent nor patient, but instrument. The Chorus know and do not know; precisely because of this they are involved in that struggle; and Eliot draws in the audience through the Chorus.

So, when the Fourth Tempter throws back Thomas's words in his face: "You know and do not know, what it is to act or suffer," he presents the Christian with the ultimate challenge of complete submission: "Now is my way clear, now is the meaning plain" means "I shall no longer act or suffer, to the sword's end." E. Martin Browne gives the most cogent interpretation of the Fourth Tempter's omission of one of the phrases which Thomas uses, "for the pattern is the action / And the suffering"; the Tempter converts the wheel from something centred around a positive and all-embracing purpose into a dead automatic mechanism, making both action and suffering meaningless forms. For Thomas—and for the Christian—both action and suffering are absolutely central to existence, and bound in with the whole process of meaning and purpose. But not action and suffering of the individual self. The point is developed in the Interlude, where Thomas says that martyrdom "is never the design of man; for the true martyr is he who has become the instrument of God, who has lost his will in the will of God, and who no longer desires anything for himself, not even the glory of being a martyr." Of course this is a statement of both Christian sentiment and doctrine. But in the way it is stated it bears a very close relationship to the underlying philosophy of the *Bhagavad Gita.* "He who seeks non-action in action. . . . / He whose every undertaking is without desire or purpose, and whose work is burnt up with the fire of knowledge, is called learned by the wise. / When he has abandoned attachment to the fruit of actions, ever contented and without support, even though he is occupied in action, he performs none."

This, then, is the subtlety and power of the Fourth Tempter who lies behind all the other three: that whereas the first three represent past stages of Thomas's being, states which Thomas has learned to recognize, the Fourth Tempter (the unexpected one) reflects Thomas's state at the present moment. Thomas forecasts the nature of the agon before it begins:

> For a little time the hungry hawk
> Will only soar and hover, circling lower,
> Waiting excuse, pretence, opportunity.
> End will be simple, sudden, God-given.
> Meanwhile the substance of our first act
> Will be shadows, and the strife with shadows.

But the Fourth Tempter defeats expectation; he is no shadow challenger, but Thomas's stubborn, continuing personal will and pride embodied in its most dangerous form. Sensual ease promised by the First Tempter; temporal power under the king, promised by the Second; power over the minds and hearts of the people, promised by the Third; these appeals to the will are easily turned aside; but even the Tempters who promise them hint at the ultimate temptation: "I leave you to the pleasures of your higher vices" says the First Tempter, and the Second, "Your sin soars sunward, covering king's falcons." The first three temptations parallel Satan's temptation of Christ in the desert to satisfy his physical hunger (Luke 4:3–4) and to enjoy the kingdoms of the world (Luke 4:5–6). The fourth exploits the lust for the spiritual power of the miracle, as Satan tempted Christ to cast Himself down from the pinnacle of the temple. The fourth temptation is to a *voluntary* martyrdom, a willed martyrdom, rather than an inevitable martyrdom as part of the grand design.

According to this pattern of ideas, then, the pathos is not strictly the suffering of Thomas; it is, however, the necessary suffering of the Chorus and the community to bring about a purgation of the world. The intimate relationship between the Chorus and Thomas is beautifully expressed by E. Martin Browne when he tells of the new discoveries which he made when playing Thomas in an "emergency version" of *Murder in the Cathedral* in the early years of the Second World War:

> His long silent struggle with despair as the Tempters sur- round him is carried on in isolation until the women succeed in breaking through to him. It is their intuition that "the Lords of Hell are here" which reveals to him the nature of his danger. It is their plea:
>
> > O Thomas Archbishop, save us, save us, save yourself that we may be saved;
> > Destroy yourself and we are destroyed.
>
> which calls forth from him the power to banish the Tempters.

But their intuition is ambiguous: in the two lines which Browne quotes from page 30 of *Collected Plays,* both "save" and "destroy" can and do bear entirely contrary meanings in a complex ambiguity— "They speak better than they know." Instinctive, unreasoning fear of the hellish forces which cling round Thomas impel them to ask for a return to the drab but secure routine which existed before Thomas's return, and to ask that he should save himself by running away. They fear their own destruction through his. But Thomas recognizes the obverse of the ambiguity, the sense in which the lines mean that only by his martyrdom, only by his destruction as a self may the women of Canterbury be destroyed and saved through destruction. The Chorus speaks of the defilement of the world by conflict at the beginning of part 2: "war among men defiles the world, but death in the Lord renews it, / And the world must be cleaned in the winter, or we shall have only / A sour spring, a parched summer, an empty harvest." Again Eliot hints at Greek myth in his Christian parable: Thomas is playing the role of *pharmakos,* the ritual scapegoat who is driven away by the peo- ple of the tribe in a symbolic purgation of evil. It is also a role which Christ plays in the drama of the mass: "Agnus dei, qui tollis peccata mundi, miserere nobis." The symbolic sacrifice of the pharmakos en- sures the success of the world's harvest; Thomas as pharmakos renews the sacrifice of Christ. But, if Thomas the individual is in one sense a functionary in a social ritual, the social ritual is also image for the drama of the individual. Thomas, like Sweeney or the male persona in *The Waste Land,* is the aspect of any soul which is capable of the ultimate spiritual adventure; he is surrounded by other aspects of any soul. The Tempters are part of him; the Chorus and the Priests are part of him, as he is of them. And the Knights are doubles of the Tempters: Eliot, on E. Martin Browne's suggestion, arranged that in the original production Knights and Tempters should be played by the same actors and, as Knights, wear a reminder of their previous appearances as Tempters. As Tempters they can harm him, for they represent the destructiveness of his own will; as Knights they cannot harm him for with the renunciation of his will he is as incapable of suffering (in his own person) as of action. But they can, and they do, continue to exercise their role as tempters. Thomas has completed his agon and won the conflict; the agon persists in the natural man, and the conflict is transferred to the audience. That is why, in the scene following the pathos, Eliot has the Knights turn round and address the audience directly, forcing the audience into total participation, challenging them to face temptation, to undergo an agon of their own. In his new role of Fourth Knight the Fourth Tempter is again the most subtle, with his question, *"Who killed the Archbishop?"* It is said that in the original performances there were murmurs of agreement at the Fourth Knight's sophistries, implicitly convicting Thomas of the gross spiritual pride of courting martyrdom, of suicide for the sake of glory. There is no wonder that this should be so; in this ironic age it is difficult to imagine any other motive than pride for such a martyrdom. The Knights represent a far more *modern* sensibility than Thomas, but Thomas acts, or Eliot makes him act, in a way which would appear insanely perverse to almost any modern audience:

> You think me reckless, desperate and mad.
> You argue by results, as this world does,
> To settle if an act be good or bad.
> You defer to the fact.

The audience is called upon, whether it knows it or not, to make a choice between two mutually incompatible standards of judgment. On the one hand, a way of judgment in which one examines and assesses cause and effect, the evidence of the senses and the probabilities suggested by experience. On the other hand a way in which judgment is reserved for God:

> It is not in time that my death shall be known;
> It is out of time that my decision is taken

If you call that decision
To which my whole being gives entire consent.
I give my life
To the Law of God above the Law of Man.

This is partly understood by the Chorus, who still lament the disturbance which they have feared since the beginning "How how can I ever return, to the soft quiet seasons?" but recognize that "this is out of life, this is out of time, / An instant eternity of evil and wrong."

Thomas's temptation is in one way a kind of Purgatory. But throughout the play the pull of Hell is felt. The interior Hell is an important theme in Eliot's verse implicit in "Prufrock," *The Waste Land* and "The Hollow Men," and explicit in plays like *The Family Reunion* and *The Cocktail Party*. The history of Hell has never been fully written: if one were to attempt to trace the changes in its geography and significance from ancient times to the present day one would be forced to write half the history of the human mind, and of the religious sensibility. At first it was another place, a distinct location, a place to be feared and abhorred, but normally beyond the living experience of humanity. A hero or a dreamer could enter Hell and return; he could triumph over the terror and return to the living world a being more than human, capable of action and of speech which could restore and refresh the world; but he would leave behind him a place which remained powerful, independent, with its own king, its own laws, its own separate reality. Some time during the Renaissance Hell began to migrate. It is always implicit in the anagogical reach of meaning of *La Divina Commedia* that Hell, like Purgatory, the earthly Paradise, and Heaven, has its place in the heart of the living human being. During and after the Renaissance man became more and more interested in himself; God became mysteriously divided, being both within man and utterly beyond him, and Hell began to lose its boundaries. Christian mysticism sought a state of being on earth as like as possible to heavenly beatitude; as a natural corollary Hell tore up its frontier treaties and became a state of mind, capable of existing wherever there was a man or angel capable of experiencing evil. The discovery of the inner Hell became most terrible for those who were torn between the religious and the humanist way of seeing. Marlowe made Mephistophiles tell Faustus:

Hell hath no limits, nor is circumscribed
In one self-place; for where we are is Hell

And where Hell is, there we must ever be.

(Doctor Faustus, sc. 5)

[Sir Thomas] Browne, in *Religio Medici* had written: "The heart of man is the place the devils dwell in: I feel sometimes a hell within myself." And Milton seemed to be well acquainted with Hell when he wrote of:

A mind not to be chang'd by place or time.
The mind is its own place, and in itself
Can make a heaven of hell, a hell of heaven.

(Paradise Lost, bk. 1)

and:

Which way shall I fly
Infinite wrath and infinite despair?
Which way I fly is hell; myself am hell;
And in the lowest deep a lower deep,
Still threat'ning to devour me, opens wide,
To which the hell I suffer seems a heaven.

(Paradise Lost, bk. 4)

In *The Cocktail Party,* the traditional motif reasserts itself in a very clear verbal reminiscence; Edward Chamberlayne says to Lavinia:

What is hell? Hell is oneself,
Hell is alone, the other figures in it
Merely projections. There is nothing to escape from
And nothing to escape to. One is always alone.

Martin Browne tells us that at the dress rehearsal of *The Cocktail Party* before the Edinburgh Festival production "Eliot leaned over and whispered: 'Contre Sartre.' The line, and the whole story of Edward and Lavinia, are his reply to 'Hell is other people' in *Huis Clos.*" Or, one might say, the response of the poet of tradition to an existentialist heterodoxy. Sartre's brand of existentialism subverts humanism by a bitter inversion; Eliot's newly humane Christianity subverts humanism equally, but by enfolding it within a religious tradition, which gains its mature strength from the tongues of the dead through seven centuries of speech, from Dante to our own troubled world.

In *Murder in the Cathedral,* the notion of the interior Hell is expressed with an unusual power and energy by the Chorus, Eliot achieving in his own way what he had praised Dante for doing, in a very different way, in the *Inferno:* "It reminds us that Hell is not a place but a *state;* that man is damned or blessed in the creatures of his imagination as well as in men who have actually lived; and that Hell, though a state, is a state which can only be thought of, and perhaps only experienced, by the projection of sensory images."

The long Chorus which begins "I have smelt them, the deathbringers" evokes this horror and sense of corruption more powerfully, perhaps, than the prophecies of Hell in *The Waste Land*—certainly far more effectively than the threadbare and miscellaneous images which Harry uses to describe the personal Hell in *The Family Reunion:* "One thinks to escape / By violence, but one is still alone / In an overcrowded desert, jostled by ghosts." Harry excuses the inefficiency of his language for describing the horror by saying "I talk in general terms / Because the particular has no language." But the Dante essay is right: Hell can only be thought of in particular terms; certainly a particularity of reference is the only way in which the horrifying conviction of the Chorus of the immanence of Hell and the obscenity which lies beneath all sensual experience can be expressed.

In one way Eliot goes further in expressing the total range of human experience than any other poet ever has done (only in one way—there are other ways in which the range of experience expressed is severely, even cripplingly, limited). While Thomas expresses the highest reaches of the human conflict, the Chorus here expresses a range of human experience in which the intellect is no longer important —a state of feeling in which the sensitive faculties are so hyperacute and so all-embracing that their experience becomes the experience of all creation. The passage stretches our sensory imaginations as far, even further than our spiritual imaginations are stretched by Thomas's martyrdom:

> I have lain on the floor of the sea and breathed with the
>> breathing of the sea anemone, swallowed with the
>> ingurgitation of the sponge. I have lain in the soil and
>> criticised the worm. In the air
> Flirted with the passage of the kite, I have plunged with the
>> kite and cowered with the wren. I have felt
> The horn of the beetle, the scale of the viper, the mobile hard
>> insensitive skin of the elephant, the evasive flank of
>> the fish.
> I have smelt

Corruption in the dish, incense in the latrine, the sewer in
     the incense, the smell of sweet soap in the woodpath,
     a hellish sweet scent in the woodpath, while the
     ground heaved. I have seen
Rings of light coiling downwards, descending
To the horror of the ape.

Even though the passage stretches to include images of exaltation, the predominating effect is of corruption and obscenity which is every bit as disturbing as the savage horror of Swift at his most destructive. The cascading freedom of the rhetoric resembles St John Perse, whom Eliot had recently translated, but the vision in all its horror is peculiarly Eliot's own. It is the natural complement of the vision of reconciliation which is expressed through Thomas's martyrdom—no vision of Heaven can exist without an equally acute vision of Hell, no exaltation of spirit without a consciousness of death which stretches beyond a personal fear into a consciousness of the horror of all creation. It is a terrible sickness that is expressed here; but then perhaps religious exaltation demands and implies a terrible sickness, an extension of the consciousness beyond the bearable limits of experience. It is "mind-bending" in the current phrase; though bending the mind need not end in permanent distortion, but in a shaping of experience into a new order better able to cope with the less dramatic but more central and stabilizing emotions which we conventionally call health.

The whole passage is the most obvious attempt Eliot ever made to fulfil the requirement which Rémy de Gourmont made of great poetry and which Eliot summarizes in his essay on the Metaphysical poets: "One must look into the cerebral cortex, the nervous system, and the digestive tracts."

What is woven on the loom of fate
What is woven in the councils of princes
Is woven also in our veins, our brains
Is woven like a pattern of living worms
In the guts of the women of Canterbury

The pattern of personae in *Murder in the Cathedral* is somewhat like the conventional pattern of the organization of the state developed by the ponderous Menenius and the first citizen in *Coriolanus*, 1.1 (following Paul in 1 Corinthians 12) in which the head, the eye, the heart, the arm of the state depend upon the seemingly inactive belly storing and sending life "through the rivers of your blood, / Even to the court, the heart, to the seat o' th' brain." It is the part of the sensuous imagination which the women of Canterbury play; and their role is as necessary to Thomas as Thomas is to them. The role is played, as we have seen, by the women of *The Waste Land,* and the triumph of the questing male persona would be their rape, desertion and death. The same curious and arresting metaphor occurs in another, equally extraordinary and disturbing form in *Murder in the Cathedral.* Here the women express their own foreboding of death in terms of rape, the experience of total humiliation and desecration of the body, but in terms which relate physical lust and spiritual longings. It's curious how Thomas himself is ambiguously implicated in the pattern of rape—for this hellish agony of the spirit is the necessary counterpart of his triumphant pathos:

> Nothing is possible but the shamed swoon
> Of those consenting to the last humiliation.
> I have consented, Lord Archbishop, have consented.
> Am torn away, subdued, violated,
> United to the spiritual flesh of nature,
> Mastered by the animal powers of spirit,
> Dominated by the lust of self-demolition,
> By the final utter uttermost death of spirit,
> By the final ecstasy of waste and shame.

The hint of Shakespeare's 129th sonnet, "The expense of spirit in a waste of shame / Is lust in action" in the last line helps to place the particular quality of the emotion in its context. Shakespeare's sonnet on the treachery of desire agrees well with the sentiment of "The Hollow Men" and *Ash-Wednesday* on the state of dream perception between memory and anticipation, "The place of solitude where three dreams cross." The sonnet ends:

> Before, a joy propos'd; behind, a dream.
> All this the world well knows; yet none knows well
> To shun the heaven that leads men to this hell.

But Thomas comforts the women of Canterbury with the assurance that this knowledge of Hell is a necessary moment, still using sexual imagery, the imagery of the orgasm, but equally the imagery of St Theresa's ecstasy, to express a resolution of Hell in knowledge of Heaven:

This is your share of the eternal burden,
The perpetual glory. This is one moment,
But know that another
Shall pierce you with a sudden painful joy
When the figure of God's purpose is made complete.

As is to be expected, the play ends with a Threnos (in which are dissolved ghostly elements of the suppressed Anagnorisis or recognition scene and Theophany or appearance of the God). As one would expect from Murray there is a clash of contrary emotions, sorrow and affirmative joy blending. Affirmation predominates: for instance the Chorus return once more to their characteristic pattern of animal imagery, not now in the horrified flinching imagination of obscene contact, but in a triumphant Gloria: even those who deny God affirm Him simply by living: "all things affirm Thee in living; the bird in the air, both the hawk and the finch; the beast on the earth, both the wolf and the lamb; the worm in the soil and the worm in the belly. / Therefore man." But affirmation is a difficult note as yet for Eliot to strike. In *Murder in the Cathedral* Hell is still known better than Heaven, and the pain of Purgatory more clearly felt than its joy.

Poetic Drama

Stephen Spender

The true theme of Eliot's plays written after his conversion is the discovery by heroes, and one heroine, of their religious vocation. It is required of the hero that he perfect his will so as to make it conform completely with the will of God. The play in which these aims are revealed in a very pure state—*naturaliter*—is *Murder in the Cathedral.* The problem of Thomas Becket is not to attain the courage necessary for him to undergo martyrdom—from his first entrance on the stage he is set on being martyred—but to purify himself of all self-regarding motives for martyrdom. His conversations with the Tempters reveal this aim.

The dramatic purpose of the First and Third Tempters is not really to tempt, since they offer Thomas choices of pleasure and political partisanship which he has already clearly rejected. Their purpose is to set before the audience images of Thomas's past—the life of personal enjoyment, friendship with the king, and temporal power. These Tempters are ghosts from that past. The Second Tempter also offers Thomas a choice he has rejected. However, this choice is not just evocative of the past, but needs to be defined and explained in order that the spectator may clearly understand Thomas's present position. It is the choice of doing material good in the temporal world, an action which Thomas, as a spiritual leader in command of temporal power, might well undertake. The Second Tempter asks him to become Chancellor again in order that he may save the people from misgovernment. Thomas has no difficulty in rejecting the part of this tempta-

From *Penguin Modern Masters: T. S. Eliot,* edited by Frank Kermode. © 1975 by Stephen Spender. Penguin, 1975.

tion which concerns covering himself in worldly glory. But a further temptation involves him in exacter definition of his aims: the temptation to use a power in order to achieve good:

> Temporal power, to build a good world,
> To keep order, as the world knows order.

Thomas rejects this on the grounds that he has made a choice beyond that of doing good in the world through power. It is that of spiritual power and carrying out the will of God.

The Third Tempter, like the first, offers a temptation which can scarcely be expected to tempt. This is for Thomas to ally himself with the English barons against the King with whom his friendship has been broken. As a temptation this is meaningless. In the terms of temporal power Thomas is on the side of the King against the barons.

Finally there is the Fourth Tempter—the only one who really tempts Thomas because he echoes what are his own thoughts, the prospects of the "enduring crown to be won" through martyrdom:

> What can compare with glory of Saints
> Dwelling forever in presence of God?
>
> . . . .
>
> Seek the way of martyrdom, make yourself the lowest
> On earth, to be high in heaven.
> And see far off below you, where the gulf is fixed,
> Your persecutors, in timeless torment,
> Parched passion, beyond expiation.

Thomas recognizes this voice as the echo of his own and knowing this he cries:

> Can sinful pride be driven out
> Only by more sinful? Can I neither act nor suffer
> Without perdition?

The hero or the martyr may be acting out of pride and the desire for glory. Glory is indeed the crown of martyrdom, but for the martyr to act on this knowledge corrupts his action and puts him on the level of those concerned with their own power and glory. The will of the individual has to be absorbed within the objective will which is the love of God so disinterestedly that action becomes passive suffering, subjectively motiveless. There are, of course, theological arguments, going back to Aristotle, and resumed by Thomas Aquinas and Dante, which discuss this. But drama concretizes abstractions as living situations, and the situation of Thomas Becket, with his tormenting doubt as to his motives, is real. We can see this for ourselves by taking the example of the Agony of Christ in the Garden of Gethsemane. If any thought had entered his mind that his crucifixion would be the most successful advertising operation in the history of Western civilization, and if this thought were any element of a motive in his action, then the pure act of submission to his enemies, in order that his will might become perfect within the love that is God, would have been corrupted, and the crucifixion would have been a kind of betrayal. It is because people see the crucifixion in the light of success and triumph that we end up with Jesus Christ Superstar (a transformation of the original Christian myth into terms of the modern world of business which corresponds perhaps to James Joyce's ironic transformation of Odysseus into Leopold Bloom).

The Fourth Tempter, having echoed and clarified for him Thomas's aspirations for the glory of martyrdom, now echoes his rejection of his own self-regard, his dedication to the aim of submerging every element of his own will within the will of God. The Fourth Tempter takes up indeed the very words that Thomas has himself spoken to the Chorus:

> You know and do not know, what it is to act or suffer.
> You know and do not know, that action is suffering,
> And suffering action. Neither does the agent suffer
> Nor the patient act. But both are fixed
> In an eternal action, an eternal patience
> To which all must consent that it may be willed
> And which all must suffer that they may will it,
> That the pattern may subsist, that the wheel may turn and still
> Be forever still.

This is a moment when Eliot merges his own poetry in what was for him the supreme moment of Dante—"in his will is our peace."

In his concluding speech of the first act, Becket moves forward spiritually into an area of lucid consciousness. The Fourth Tempter, echo of his own wishes (and perhaps his angel in the same way that Satan is the angel sent forth by God to tempt Job), has shown him his own heart's way to purge his soul of impure motivation:

> Now is my way clear, now is the meaning plain:
> Temptation shall not come in this kind again.

> The last temptation is the greatest treason:
> To do the right deed for the wrong reason.

The first three Tempters are now seen as visitations from the past, "ghosts" (like Gomez and Mrs. Carghill in *The Elder Statesman*). They are the occasion for a review of his past as friend of the King, and for confrontation with the fact that spiritual authority puts the soul in even deadlier danger than temporal power:

> For those who serve the greater cause may make the cause
> serve them,
> Still doing right: and striving with political men
> May make that cause political, not by what they do
> But by what they are.

Thomas, addressing out of his past a "modern" audience, knows that his history will seem futile to most of these onlookers, the lunatic self-slaughter of a fanatic. His aim is further elucidated in the sermon which he preaches in the cathedral on Christmas morning, 1170:

> A Christian martyrdom is no accident. Saints are not made
> by accident. . . . A martyr, a saint, is always made by the
> design of God, for His love of men, to warn them and to
> lead them, to bring them back to His ways. A martyrdom is
> never the design of man; for the true martyr is he who has
> become the instrument of God, who has lost his will in the
> will of God. . . . The martyr no longer desires anything for
> himself, not even the glory of martyrdom.

This way of thinking, culminating in his religion, had fundamentally been Eliot's since the discussion of the relation of the living poet to the whole past tradition in the essay on "Tradition and the Individual Talent." The poet is seen not as expressing his own personality but as surrendering and even extinguishing it within the objective life which is the tradition. The relation of the subjective individual who has found his vocation to an impersonal objective life is sacrificial. Eliot has found beyond literature, beyond the tradition, that further life which, in his view, creates living values.

The Four Knights, agents of the King, who come to murder Thomas and who explain at considerable length, in a style that owes something to Shaw's *St. Joan,* their reasons for doing so, correspond to the Four Tempters. In a sense they are indeed Tempters, not of Thomas but of the Chorus in seeking their approbation of the murder. They are also, just as much as Thomas, instruments whereby Thomas perfects his own will within that of God. Although agents of ultimate good, they are, nevertheless, wicked not only before God but in the temporal world. As Archbishop of Canterbury, Thomas Becket, their opponent, is a doughty champion of the war of the spiritual authority against the temporal powers, whether of the King or of the barons, in his time.

It is a very fine stroke whereby Eliot makes Thomas, a few seconds before his assassination, recover his sense of his real authority in the world, which derives from his office and from Rome, and rebuke one of the Knights who calls him traitor. He cries:

> You, Reginald, three times traitor you:
> Traitor to me as my temporal vassal,
> Traitor to me as your spiritual lord,
> Traitor to God in desecrating His Church.

The Women of Canterbury are not wicked but vacillating, concerned with their own interest but capable of accepting the burden of participating in a drama which can offer them nothing but the worsening of their own material conditions. Their poetry is perhaps the greatest triumph of *Murder in the Cathedral.* It is unparalleled in Eliot's work.

The choruses of *The Rock* are preparatory exercises for it, but tend to provide examples either of spiritual exhortation (which does not fit well in the mouths of a chorus of common folk who are being exhorted) or of Eliot's mysticism. In *The Rock* Eliot is incapable of giving expression to the feelings of ordinary modern men and women, because he cannot see them except as corrupted by the time. It is only when, in *The Family Reunion,* he enters into the feelings of the English upper middle class that he can to some extent voice them because they appertain to the unnerved, divided, guilt-ridden, past-conscious English culture by which he himself has been adopted.

The Women of Canterbury are another matter. Eliot can see them as rooted in rituals of toil—rituals of the seasons—as sharing the dignity of their domestic and agricultural labor, as having their place within a hierarchy whose temporal head is the King and whose spiritual head is the Archbishop, representative of the Pope in Rome. Eliot's picture of the people of Canterbury may not be historically exact but it is imaginatively moving. He is able to visualize their lives within the context of values and conflicts which the play is about. They obey the King. They go to Church. They work. They are afraid of the barons. They

are therefore capable of commenting on the action which they first
obscurely, and later luminously, understand. They are in a relation to
Thomas which is that both of chorus and of a generalized protagonist
capable of entering into a dialogue with him.

In the magnificent series of choruses which follow on the declaration by the Knights of their intent to kill the Archbishop, Eliot,
through these voices of the past, focuses his feelings of horror in a
universal vision which includes the present as well as the past:

> Clear the air! clean the sky! wash the wind! take stone from
> stone and wash them.
> The land is foul, the water is foul, our beasts and ourselves
> defiled with blood.
> A rain of blood has blinded my eyes. Where is England?
> where is Kent? where is Canterbury?
> O far far far far in the past; and I wander in a land of barren
> boughs: if I break them, they bleed; I wander in a land
> of dry stones: if I touch them they bleed.

Eliot here touches the utmost depths of horror that he knows, which
we find in "Prufrock," *The Waste Land, Sweeney Agonistes*—indeed,
throughout his work. But whereas in the earlier poetry the horror
seems cut off, unrelated, an individual's nightmare, here it seems
brought up into a light capable ultimately indeed of cleaning the sky
and washing the wind.

No one knows better than Eliot the horror of waking in the uncertain hour between darkness and the first dawn of an icy gritty day in
Paris or London; of unswept corners of attics; of funguses that grow
behind dark wainscoting; of a cat in an alley gutter licking the inside of
a sardine tin; of the war between clawed enemies that takes place under
rocks fathoms down on the sea floor. There is a remarkable list of the
infinitesimal glimpsed terrors that surround us throughout our lives
and which burrow through our flesh in these choruses:

> I have tasted
> The living lobster, the crab, the oyster, the whelk and the
> prawn; and they live and spawn in my bowels, and
> my bowels dissolve in the light of dawn. I have smelt
> Death in the rose, death in the hollyhock, sweet pea,
> hyacinth, primrose and cowslip. I have seen
> Trunk and horn, tusk and hoof, in odd places;

> I have lain on the floor of the sea and breathed with the
> breathing of the sea-anemone, swallowed with
> ingurgitation of the sponge. I have lain in the soil and
> criticised the worm. In the air
> Flirted with the passage of the kite, I have plunged with the
> kite and cowered with the wren. I have felt
> The horn of the beetle, the scale of the viper, the mobile
> hard insensitive skin of the elephant, the evasive
> flank of the fish.

This is to make the whole animal world and all its processes corrupt, whether they operate outside us or within our bodies, in the elements or in the intestines, a vast psalm of life metabolistically changing into death surrounding human beings and happening inside them.

Nietzsche thought that the genius of Wagner was as a miniaturist, an observer of minutiae which make the spirit most uneasy, with the gifts of a painter of Dutch interiors; and that his mistake was to compose on the scale of epic grandeur. The most real horror that Eliot conveys in his work is also in the isolated phrase suspended between commas, as in the early "Preludes" and "Rhapsody on a Windy Night." Eliot, a poet of fragments skilfully dovetailed into wholes, is a miniaturist. He is more immediately convincing when conveying the terror inspired by a spider in its web in the corner of an attic, by cigarette butts on the unswept floor of a bar at dawn, than at comparing the case of bad conscience of a retired businessman with that of Oedipus at Colonus, or the sense of guilt of a young man who thinks he has pushed his wife overboard an ocean liner, with that of Orestes pursued by the Eumenides.

There is indeed some affinity between Eliot and Wagner. Once, after having followed a radio performance of *Das Rheingold* with the score, I asked him whether, when he wrote *The Waste Land,* he had been studying this libretto. He looked at me slyly and said: "Not just *Rheingold*—the whole of the Ring."

Die Meistersinger is probably Wagner's opera which is most successful as a work of art, precisely because it is woven out of scenes like paintings by some Dutch master. Wagner's vision of medieval Nuremberg is of a society which forms an organic unity. Eliot can enter into the conflicts of Canterbury in the year 1170 because the struggle between the temporal and the spiritual powers—within the context of a society in which heaven and hell were regarded as real places—is one that he can imagine. In *Murder in the Cathedral* he does not have to resort to the Joycean device of the parallel myth taken from antiquity which he applies to *The Waste Land* and which can with some effort be interpreted as parallels from Greek tragedy in his later dramas.

Murder in the Cathedral:
The Countersacramental Play of Signs

Michael T. Beehler

William Spanos concludes his careful study of *The Christian Tradition in Modern British Verse Drama* with the observation that "the Christian verse drama movement has definitively, if only broadly, established the sacramental aesthetic as its operative principle and thus has acknowledged the integrity of the dramatic image." Earlier in his book, Spanos outlines this "operative principle" that he finds so fundamental to this particular genre. Deriving his position from Erich Auerbach's exhaustive study of the origins and uses of figural interpretation, Spanos notes that the sacramental vision presented by Christian verse drama "reconciles the concrete reality and value that the empirical world dichotomizes; and, in so doing, it rescues value from naturalistic and reality from idealistic art." Utilizing the dramatic potential of *figura,* the plays of this genre present a universe in which "all objects in space (nature) and all events in time (history) are placed according to a universal scheme and given transcendent significance." Thus by interpreting history from a sacramental or figural perspective, "history itself becomes a *figura,* concrete yet figurative; in short, symbolic."

In this manner, then, the sacramental perspective seeks to redeem the signs of history, and to present them as having an extra-historical value and significance. As Spanos points out, the historical sign, for the "realist," "has no transcendent meaning," and thus history itself appears as a "linear progression (or recession) [of signs that are]... devoid of spiritual significance or value, and, therefore, of authentic

From *Genre* 10, no. 3 (Fall 1977). © 1977 by the University of Oklahoma.

poetry." But the sacramental aesthetic attempts to resolve this recessive play of meaningless signs by seeing history from a perspective in which every "moment in history, every human action, is infused by a discoverable universal and permanent significance without loss of its unique actuality, its historicity." In short, the signs of history appear as faithful, proper figures of a transcendent significance, an "eternal present" discoverable in the historical sign itself. Thus the "operative principle" of the sacramental aesthetic seems to produce a conjunctive effect, an apparent joining of "time and eternity, the many and the one, motion and stillness... concrete reality and value." This effect is accurately described by Lévi-Strauss's term "ritual," for it "brings about a union... or in any case an organic relation between two initially separate groups" (*The Savage Mind,* tr. George Weidenfeld and Nicolson Ltd.). Beginning with the apparent difference between the historical sign and an eternal significance, Christian verse drama, through the sacramental aesthetic, seeks to restore a symmetrical unity.

Spanos sees in Eliot's *Murder in the Cathedral* a "significant development in the art of the Christian verse drama," for this play, like the subsequent Christian Histories commissioned by the Friends of Canterbury, utilizes this "sacramental concept of time... as a genuine aesthetic." This sacramental aesthetic is thus a "necessary condition of perceiving the continuity of Eliot's efforts in the poetic drama," and Spanos characterizes *Murder in the Cathedral* itself as a play that employs this aesthetic in an attempt to reconcile and reintegrate "all the irreconcilables of life in naturalistic time... into a great sacramental image of the eternal design." But although Eliot's play seeks to achieve such an ultimate unity through an apparently ritualistic movement, its desired resolution is nevertheless undercut by an obverse movement that is coincident with the ritual itself, and that ultimately calls into question its supposedly conjunctive effect. Like the one described by Spanos, this other movement takes place in the historical sign itself, but its effect is that of a game rather than a ritual: that is, instead of resolving the difference between the historical sign and a "discoverable universal and permanent significance," this movement forever defers the presentation of this "eternal present." Its effect is thus disjunctive rather that conjunctive, and the historical sign, rather than marking the presence of an "eternal design," marks rather that design's abysmal absence. *Murder in the Cathedral* traces this movement in the sign, and continually plays its game of deferral.

The process of figural interpretation, which Spanos shows to be fundamental to the genre of Christian verse drama, underwrites this deferring play. As Auerbach points out, the historical event is unalterably an incomplete sign: "Figural prophecy implies the interpretation of one worldly event through another; the first signifies the second, the second fulfills the first. Both remain historical events; yet both, looked at in this way, have something provisional and incomplete about them; they point to one another and both point to something in the future, something still to come, which will be the actual, real, and definitive event." Thus the historical sign remains "provisional and incomplete" as long as the "real" event from which it presumably derives its significance remains absent. Because of this missing event, "history, with all its concrete force, remains forever a figure, cloaked and needful of interpretation . . . all history . . . remains open and questionable, [and] points to something still concealed" (" 'Figura,' " in *Scenes from the Drama of European Literature*). In other words, the historical sign, rather than revealing a transcendent significance that will supposedly resolve and complete it, instead insures that a final "real" event will remain forever concealed by a falsifying figure. It "points to" this event only by presenting itself as an aberration; hence the event can never "appear" as such, but can be thought only as an unknowable term which the figure forever deflects or holds in reserve. For this reason, history does not become an "eternal present," but is rather "forever a figure," a labyrinthine *mise en abyme* in which no transcendent significance, no presence, is discoverable. The perpetual deferral of any resolving significance is in fact the fundamental condition for the appearance of the historical sign. This idea is implicit in Auerbach's observation that "purely spiritual elements enter into the conceptions of the ultimate fulfillment [of the historical sign], since 'my kingdom is not of this world'; yet it will be a real kingdom, not an immaterial abstraction; only the *figura,* not the *natura* will pass away." The signs of history "pass away" in the presence of presence: they therefore arise only in its absence, and are maintained only by its perpetual deferral. Thus figural interpretation, which arises from the desire to resolve the differences of history into a transcendent, unified significance, itself engenders difference by unavoidably deferring a "real" event, and thereby continually opening up the historical sign to the play of interpretation. This play can be only figuratively closed by a "spiritual act" of faith that supplements with an interpretation (i.e., another figure) the absence at the sign's center.

It is this unsponsored and eccentric play in the historical sign that problematizes the ritualistic, sacramental vision of Christian verse drama in general and of *Murder in the Cathedral* in particular. As E. Martin Browne points out, Eliot's drama is an attempt to "celebrate the cult associated with a sacred spot by displaying the story of its origin." In order to display this "origin," Eliot must deal with an historical event: the death of Thomas Becket. Several earlier writers, most notably Tennyson and George Darley, had dealt with this event from a fundamentally historical point of view, but it is precisely this point of view which becomes problematic for Eliot. As the Knights' speeches at the end of part 2 suggest, Becket's death, when seen from a strictly historical perspective, suffers from an excess of signification, for it presents an excess of meanings over which no single meaning has authority. The Knights offer three conflicting interpretations of the event: for the Second Knight, the murder was necessary to subordinate the Church to the State; for the Fourth Knight, Becket's death was not a murder, but was rather a "Suicide while of Unsound Mind"; and for the Third Knight, it was merely the natural result of the play of historical forces. Murder, suicide, or natural death? These interpretations of Becket's demise are irreconcilable: as Thomas himself indicates, every historical event is doubled: "For every life and every act / Consequences of good and evil can be shown." At the close of the first part, he explains that, from an historical perspective, his death will appear to be an unauthorized sign, and will call forth an abysmal play or excess of meaning:

> I know
> What yet remains to show you of my history
> Will seem to most of you at best futility,
> Senseless self-slaughter of a lunatic,
> Arrogant passion of a fanatic.

It is this historical abyss which Eliot must supply with a bottom, a ground. By displaying the authentic "origin" of the cult, he would presumably resolve this temporal game of differences into the unity of a sacramental ritual.

Becket is himself no less a sign of an excess of meaning than is his death. The play is in fact partly a struggle over the right of any single authority (barons, Church, King) to appropriate Becket as its proper sign. As the play begins, the Second Priest expects that Becket's return will restore to Canterbury its authentic father, its truly authorizing presence who

> shall be at our head, dispelling dismay and doubt.
> He will tell us what we are to do, he will give us our orders,
> 	instruct us.
> 	. . . .
> 	when the Archbishop returns
> Our doubts are dispelled.

But as it continues, the play exhibits this authorizing presence as a problematic sign. According to the Three Knights, Becket is the "Archbishop who was made by the King; whom he set in [his] place to carry out his command." He must therefore transact "[the King's] business in his absence": in short, he must be a sign of the King, and stand for him when he is not present. But Becket, as the Three Knights also point out, is a sign "in revolt against the King," and this revolt is figured by his assumption of an additional signification, one which is in excess of the King, and which occurs in his absence. Although he was "made by the King," he presents himself in part 2 as the sign of the Church: "It is not Becket who pronounces doom, / But the Law of Christ's Church, the judgment of Rome." Thus both Becket and his death reflect the problematic of the historical sign. Instead of displaying the simple origin of the cult of Canterbury, these signs, when viewed from an historical perspective, reveal history's bottomless chasm. They appear not as the proper signs of an authorizing presence, but rather as marks of an excess of signification, and therefore of a potentially infinite substitutability; one interpretation displacing another, each substituting itself into the place of the king in a game which forever defers the possibility of an authentic king. As the First Tempter says in part 1, "When one king is dead, there's another king, / And one more king is another reign." In *Murder in the Cathedral,* there is no rest for the signifier which is at play in history, "no rest in the house" of signification.

It is clear, then, why Eliot must replace this historical perspective with a sacramental one: he must stop the play of substitutions which takes place within the signs of the cult's origin. This displacement and substitution is figured by the play's implicit rejection of the Knights' rationalizations, and also by Becket's explicit refutation of the first three Tempters. These figures not only tempt Becket with "the good time," "power," and "treachery" against the King, but more importantly, as Spanos has pointed out, they "orient Thomas's vision in the direction of the past, the present, and the future, that is, on the level of time." By rejecting them, Becket rejects "historical time or the world in its three temporal manifestations," a gesture which marks Eliot's displacement of a purely temporal interpretation of historical signs. This displacement enables Eliot to supplement the historical accounts of Becket's death, which rely upon the various interpretations of the eyewitnesses, with texts from other sources, and results in a "novel and peculiarly unhistorical treatment of the protagonist's character." The supplementation of the historical perspective on Becket's death by a sacramental point of view marks Eliot's desire for an authorizing presence, a desire born from the "indefinite multiplication" figured by the *mise en abyme* of the historical sign. For Eliot, as for the priests, this presence "must not be absent from the divine office" which is presumably its sign. Like the Chorus, Eliot shrinks from "the empty land / Which is no land [the bottomless abyss of history], only emptiness, absence, the Void."

Thus the play shifts its emphasis away from the historical moment of Becket's death and onto that moment in part 1 when Thomas avoids the "greatest treason" of the "last temptation" ("To do the right deed for the wrong reason") . . . and presumably places his will in line with the divine will. It is this moment, in which Becket decides to allow the "right deed" to happen for the right "reason," that is in fact the origin of the cult of Canterbury which Eliot desires to display, for it is by this decision, and not simply by his death (which appears as an abysmal excess of "reasons"), that Becket qualifies himself for sainthood. This is, for Eliot, the moment that authorizes Becket's death; a moment which reenacts the full presence of the Incarnation, and recalls the Word-made-Flesh that delimits the play of significations within the historical sign. But as Hugh Kenner points out, this moment of the "purification of Becket's will," which is the "main moral action of the play," is "insufficiently analyzed." Kenner understates the problem here, for this moment of origin, this moment of full presence which authorizes the historical sign, cannot present itself as such. The play displays it here only as a silence (Becket's silence) over which the Chorus, the Tempters, and the Priests speak their various interpretations. When the moment finally breaks into speech, that is, when Becket returns to the stage and exclaims, "Now is my way clear, now is the meaning plain, that speech is already belated: Becket's "now" marks the not-now of the moment of full presence: his "now," always coming after, designates the *then* of the moment which is not *now* present. Thus the moment which supposedly authorizes the historical sign is itself silent: it has no sign which is coincident with it. Its silence is the absence of signs; a muteness which marks the sign's death.

The silence of the moment locks it outside of history, guaranteeing its immunity from the contamination of the sign in history's labyrinth. Outside of time, however, it can neither be heard nor seen: in short, it cannot be thought or known. As Becket himself observes, "It is not in time that my death shall be known." For this reason, the moment of full presence, occurring in part 1, requires the historical sign, Becket's death in part 2, in order to appear: being outside of time (or silent in time), it requires an outside to itself (the sign in time) in order to be made plain. Becket's death in part 2 thus supplements (belatedly) the silent moment of part 1, and is the condition for the breaking-into-appearance of that moment's presence. But as we have already seen, this death also marks the continual loss of authorizing presence in the perpetual play which takes place in the *mise en abyme* of the historical sign. This sign in history, which supplements the silent moment of full presence and is the condition for its breaking into appearance, is therefore dangerous to that presence itself, for it always designates its loss. Presence itself does not appear (as such, by itself) apart from the sign without which it cannot be known, yet that sign marks the moment of its inevitable disappearance, and hence maintains it as that which can never be known. It therefore "appears" only under erasure, as a disappearance; a silent and empty space at the center of the sign.

But it is precisely this central absence which allows the historical sign to appear, for, as we have seen, the sign dies (disappears) in the presence of the silent presence. The Chorus recognizes this in part 1. There it explicitly defines itself as a sign which must "bear witness" to the impending castastrophe in the cathedral. It awaits the return of Becket, the Father who as the lord of Canterbury will be the "rock" which will provide a "firm foothold / Against the perpetual wash of tides of balance of forces of barons and landholders": that is, he will be the authorizing presence that will resolve the turning world (like that of *Ash-Wednesday*) which is the life of the Chorus. But for the Chorus this resolution spells death, for it will bring a "doom on the house, a doom on yourself, a doom on the world." As a sign in the world of history, the Chorus requires for its existence the absence of the authorizing father. It therefore urges Thomas to "return to France," to "set the white sail" between itself as sign and Becket as father. As the Chorus indicates, the "house" (sign) of presence must be empty to stand.

Like the Chorus, the play itself reenacts in its own central section, the "Interlude," the necessary spacing figured by the "white sail." This moment of rhetoric (Becket's sermon) stands between the silent moment of presence in part 1 and the belated sign of absence in part 2. It therefore marks the fault between the sign and that presence on which the sign would supervene, thereby guaranteeing the sign's belatedness and designating its difference from the desired presence. This Interlude, a "white sail" of spacing in time, thus originates history itself. By requiring that the sign be different from the presence which would authorize it, and by deferring that presence by rendering its sign forever temporally belated, this interval maintains the life of the historical sign which, without it, would die in the presence of presence. By the same deferring gesture, however, this interval allows presence to be thought, for the mute presence of part 1 is manifested only as an absence in the historical sign of part 2. This sign is therefore itself a supplement which fills a void, and is constituted only by the "anterior default of a presence." Appearing as a disappearance, the presence that Eliot desires to display as the authorizing origin of both the Canterbury cult and his play thus discloses itself in that play as a nonorigin, a presence which did not simply disappear, but one which was never constituted except reciprocally (as a cancellation) by the interval itself. As the Third Priest observes, it is "only in retrospection, selection," that is, only in the deferral of presence which allows for the memorial signs of history, that "We say, that was the day."

Murder in the Cathedral thus traces Eliot's desire for a presence which would authorize the signs of history by halting their recessive play, but it is at the same time a gesture which forever defers the return of presence, marking it as always already absent. It is a play that reenacts the play of the historical sign which is endlessly enamored of a "king" against whom it is simultaneously in constant rebellion, for it memorializes the perpetually deferred becoming-present of that king. It therefore reenacts the murder which takes place in the interval, an original violence which initiates the play of history, a "Death . . . [which] also inaugurates life." This dying-away of the trace of a presence in the interval which is its origin insures that the sign will always be a "patched up affair," one that is forever "Weaving a fiction which unravels" as it is woven. It is this unavoidably doubled and counter-sacramental gesture of weaving/unweaving which keeps the game of history open and the sign in play by perpetually deferring the time of full presence when "the figure of God's purpose is made complete."

This authorizing moment of presence is therefore itself the "pattern" or "figure" which the historical sign unravels in its desire to display its own origin and to disentangle its own abysmal history. The sign produces this fictional time and figures it as the moment of its own necessarily deferred disappearance or death; a trope that it insinuates into the blank central space upon which it is itself constituted. A figure of a figure which is always deferred, this is the sign at play in history. *Murder in the Cathedral* thus reenacts this play of the sign, a play that itself enacts the doubled gesture in which presence is forever being born/killed, presented/deferred. This play stages itself in the void of the interval, the endlessly deferring Interlude in which "we celebrate at once the Birth of Our Lord and His Passion and Death."

Murder in the Cathedral: A "Liturgy Less Divine"

Robert W. Ayers

Both his critical pronouncements and his literary productions attest to T. S. Eliot's interest in the relationship of drama to Christian liturgy. If the interlocutor "E" in "A Dialogue on Dramatic Poetry" may be—as he usually is—supposed to express Eliot's personal opinion, by 1928 Eliot had come to feel that "the consummation of the drama, the perfect and ideal drama, is to be found in the ceremony of the Mass." By 1935 that feeling had assumed such shaping power that the Mass and the general Christian liturgy appear to have determined the very form of *Murder in the Cathedral*. The influence is so fundamental there that the work finally comes to be what "B" in the "Dialogue" says we crave, a "liturgy less divine [than the Mass]"—in fact, a liturgical act intended, like the Mass and the whole of the liturgy, to celebrate the glory of God.

The fulfillment of this profoundly liturgical purpose required a transmutation from dramatic to liturgical form; and that transmutation is accomplished by a virtual incorporation of the liturgy—through a multitude of liturgical texts and allusions, a comprehensive liturgical patterning of the action, and the conversion of the audience of the drama into a worshipping congregation. We must be aware of this metamorphosis if we would understand the structure, the dominant theme, and the purpose of the drama which expresses more directly

From *Texas Studies in Literature and Language* 20, no. 4 (Winter 1978). ©1978 by the University of Texas Press.

than any other the seriousness of Eliot's mind, the depth of his religious scholarship, and the quality and precision of his verse.

But in order to consider the relationships between *Murder in the Cathedral* and the liturgy, we must first confront some distinctions relating to form and purpose. A play is an unfolding process presented by actors who impersonate the characters in a story, an action addressed to the emotions or intellect of an audience, and so intended for its entertainment or edification. Since it is enacted for an audience, an audience is required; the performance of a play without an audience is a mere rehearsal. On the other hand, as a liturgical action the Mass is an action with a fixed and familiar structure, directed not to a human audience but to God, an action performed for the glory of God, and affecting the will of its participants. The Mass is both commemorative and prophetic; it incorporates within itself past actions of the same essential structure as *origins* and future actions of the same essential structure as *ends,* so completing and fulfilling itself in a continuing present, and effecting as end what it signifies as means.

A tension between these two forms—dramatic and ritual—lies at the very center of *Murder in the Cathedral;* and, in fact, the tension was given in the very decision to write a drama on the subject of martyrdom. As Thomas suggests in the Interlude, the death of a martyr is a "smaller figure" of the death of Christ; a drama on that subject is therefore likely to be a "smaller figure" of the Mass, the reenactment of Christ's sacrifice. While the subject thus attracted liturgical treatment, still a drama is to be distinguished from a Mass. In the "Dialogue on Dramatic Poetry," "B" refers this distinction to the radical of participation, saying that "a devout person, in assisting at Mass, is not in the frame of mind of a person attending a drama, for he is *participating*— and that makes all the difference."

The work was written not for performance in the theatre, but for presentation in the "semi-liturgical setting" of the Chapter House at the Canterbury Festival, June 1935. And the possibility that Eliot was employing a liturgical form for those religious precincts on that occasion of religious celebration may first occur when we observe that the Interlude in the drama is a sermon in a Mass, and that the congregation Thomas addresses in the Mass is the audience witnessing the drama. The structure implies that the drama the audience witnesses is the Mass in which the sermon exists. Once this relationship is remarked, we can recognize that the outline of the drama conforms in certain general ways to that of the Mass. In this drama, as in a Mass, of course, there are two parts separated by a sermon. The first part of the Mass, called the Mass of the Catechumens or the Liturgy of the Word, is instructional and preparational in character, and confession and repentance are dominant themes as the priest and the congregation examine their consciences in order to determine whether their attitude is worthy of participation in the sacrifice to come. Like the Mass of the Catechumens, part 1 of *Murder in the Cathedral* is all "speech," and dwells generally on the themes of confession and repentance. Here, as a consequence of confrontation with the Tempters, Thomas succeeds in "cleansing [his] lips" so that he may "worthily proclaim" the gospel of Christ in the sermon. Following the sermon, part 2 of the drama, like the second part of the Mass—called the Mass of the Faithful or the Liturgy of the Eucharist, arranged according to the order followed by Christ Himself at the Last Supper, and celebrated in commemoration of Him—is concerned with the offer of the sacrifice (Offertory), the sacrifice itself (Consecration), and the participation of the community in the sacrifice (Communion). Thus, both the structural identification of Interlude and sermon, and episodic and thematic parallels in parts 1 and 2 seem to stress Mass-form and Mass-function in the drama. Still, as we shall see, there are such differences as to mark the form of part 1 as dramatic, with the potential for dramatic development.

Returning now, and more particularly, to the beginning of the Mass and the drama, we observe that the Prayers at the Foot of the Altar prepare a congregation which has gathered in an apprehensive mood to witness the Coming of Christ in the Mass. This mood, expressed in the server's words, "Why hast thou forgotten me? Why go I mourning because of the oppression of the enemy?" is echoed by the priest, "Why art thou cast down, O my soul? And why art thou disquieted in me?" The same mood occurs in the opening of the drama, where the Women of Canterbury, having "suffered various oppression" are drawn by "some presage of an act / Which [their] eyes are compelled to witness." Sensing that "some malady is coming upon [them]," they "fear disturbance of the quiet seasons," the "winter . . . bringing death," the "ruinous spring," and "disastrous summer." But, whereas the opening chorus is in some ways similar to a processional hymn, its dominant thought is the very antithesis of that embodied in the Introit for the first Sunday of Advent, for instance; instead of expressing man's humble trust in God, as does the Introit antiphon (Psalm 25:1–4), the Chorus complains that it is *forced* to bear witness, and associates itself with Peter's denial of Christ. And rather than praying for divine guidance and enlightenment, as in the Psalm ("Shew me thy ways, O Lord; teach me thy paths"), they, who perfunctorily have "kept the feasts, heard the masses," are "content if we are left alone," passive and isolated.

The priests who speak immediately after the opening chorus are like deacons preparing for the celebrant to enter the church, and the role of the acolyte who precedes him in the Mass is performed by the Messenger, "sent before in haste / To give. . .notice of his coming." The entrance of the celebrant himself marks the Introit, the beginning of the Mass-action properly considered; so here the entrance of Archbishop Becket begins the dramatic action of the work. And his first word, significantly, is "Peace"—a translation of a bishop's salutation to his congregation, "pax vobis" (to be distinguished from the ordinary priest's "Dominus vobiscum").

In the Confiteor of the Mass, the celebrant next reflects upon his sins, acknowledges his fallibility and unworthiness in the face of temptation, and requests the intercession before God of Mary and the saints. So in the drama, Thomas prepares for the coming sacrifice by a period of self-examination; through his rejection of selfish motives and of attachment to past or future as represented in the Tempters, he will finally become one to whom "temptation shall not come in this kind again."

The Kyrie, which follows the Confiteor, and is a communal petition to the Trinity for mercy, does not appear at this point in the drama, but later, as we shall see. While at first surprising, the displacement is appropriate and derives from the distinction between the fixed ritual action of the Mass and developmental dramatic action of the play. Since the Mass is holy, commemorative, and ritualistic, its participants know before the present sacrifice that it has been enacted uncounted times before and that it will be enacted yet uncounted times to come, so that all can confidently confess their sins and implore the mercy of a God who has a proven power to absolve sins. But the basis of drama is a linear unfolding and a gradual understanding of events as they occur, so that a Kyrie would violate the logic of drama. Dramatically, the martyrdom of Thomas is unexpected; the Chorus does not yet recognize Thomas as a spiritual savior, nor—as the Women of Canterbury imply in their anguished plea to Thomas to "save yourself that we may be saved"—do they suppose his death to be inevitable and in fact necessary. Only later and gradually do they apprehend the unavoidability of Thomas's sacrifice, its identification with Christ's, and the incorporation of both into the action of the Mass.

Following the Kyrie in the Mass, and in preparation for the Gospel, we would expect the Gloria, a hymn of thanksgiving and praise in which the church gives thanks to God "for thy great glory." Since God made all things for Himself, all creatures have as their chief end the glorification of their Creator. An existential and unconscious testimony or witness is all that is possible to nonintelligent creatures, but the gift of intellect both enables and requires intelligent creatures consciously to praise the majesty and glory of the Creator manifested in the universe; as the Chorus, later become the Choir, will declare, "Man, whom Thou hast made to be conscious of Thee, must consiously praise Thee, in thought and in word and in deed." It is precisely this obligatory conscious witness to the glory of God given formal, corporate, and public expression, which produces the liturgy—and, indeed, as we shall later urge, this drama.

In the drama, the joyful response of the Chorus and the priests to the arrival of Thomas might suggest a Gloria, but this reaction is misplaced and misdirected, since it is addressed, not to God, but to Thomas as supposed temporal savior. Later, the Second Tempter's ironic offer of "the power and the glory" of political authority, and the Fourth Tempter's beguiling of Thomas with thoughts of "glory of Saints / Dwelling forever in presence of God," intimates an even more profane and perverted Gloria, in which Thomas is egocentrically tempted to witness not to God's glory, but to his own.

This, taken with Thomas's statement that he expected three visitors, not four, reveals to us that Thomas is imitating Christ, playing the role, in a profane dramatic action. Both Kyrie and Gloria are missing in the Mass-action of part 1 of the drama, then, because at this point none of the actors is yet ready to acknowledge his absolute dependence upon God; consequently, the gospel and epistle messages found throughout part 1 are either lost on an unheeding people, or used to glorify Thomas, not God. Thus, while there are numerous liturgical texts employed in liturgical sequence and form in part 1, the "rites," such as they are, are "maimed" and misdirected.

We have already seen that drama and Mass are structurally identified in the Interlude-sermon. As is usual with a sermon, this one instructs the congregation in the meaning of the liturgical action of the sacrifice, and takes as its text Luke 2:14, the gospel for the first Mass at midnight on Christmas Day and—strikingly—the opening words of the displaced Gloria: "Gloria to God in the highest and on earth peace to men of good will." Moreover, Thomas discourses upon this text in terms of the three interrelated themes of the Gloria—the praise and glorification of God, the consequent peace to men of good will, and the uniting reality between these two, the redemption by Christ. Thomas describes the death of a martyr as "a smaller figure" of the Passion of Christ; therefore, he says, on the occasion of the death of a martyr "we rejoice, that another soul is numbered among the Saints in Heaven, for the glory of God and for the salvation of men." So the sermon gives voice to the same message as the epistle for the Feast of St. Thomas [à Becket], that

> every high priest taken from among men is ordained for men in things pertaining to God, that he may offer both gifts and sacrifice for sins; who can have compassion on the ignorant, and on them that are out of the way; for that he himself also is compassed with infirmity. And by reason hereof he ought, as for the people, so also for himself, to offer for sins. And no man taketh this honor unto himself, but he that is called of God. . . . So also Christ glorified not himself to be made a high priest; but he that said unto him, "Thou art My Son, today have I begotten Thee."
>
> (Heb. 5:1-6)

If the sermon provides the most obvious identification of drama with Mass, it also provides the thematic focal point of the drama. It not only explains Thomas's rejection of the Fourth Tempter in part 1 and his ultimate self-abnegation, but also prepares the congregation for his martyrdom in part 2 and implies that he is about to offer himself to God, not in a symbolic and unbloody sense, but in an actual and bloody sense—and now with no thought for his own glory, but "for the glory of God and for the salvation of men." This in turn enables him to recognize the essentially Christlike—i.e., typological—pattern of his own surrender of will, and its relationship to "our masses" and "these our Christian mysteries." That is to say, he now understands that, like Christ's willing or suffering or consenting in Gethsemane that God's will be done, the Passion perpetually reenacted in the "mystery of our masses" is paradoxically the essential Christian action. He has come to know that action and suffering, although apparently opposite modes of conduct, are actually identical, and so at length to perceive

> that action is suffering,
> And suffering action. Neither does the agent suffer

> Nor the patient act. But both are fixed
> In an eternal action, an eternal patience
> To which all must consent that it may be willed
> And which all must suffer that they may will it.

This leads him to the more general perception that the participation of all things, even opposites, in a single pattern is necessary to the realization of God's design, the sanctification of all things, that His glory may be displayed in all the creatures of the earth, declared both in the hunter and the hunted, even in that which denies Him, as darkness declares the glory of light. Apprehending this universal pattern, Thomas knows that the evil of the Knights whose arrival he anticipates must paradoxically bring about good, that from calamity his own murder will be transfigured into a Mass—a cleansing mercy of blood, a means of redemption. Finally, since the audience witnessing the drama of Thomas is addressed as a congregation of Christians assembled for worship at a Mass, the sermon introduces the potential for a transmutation of the remaining action from a dramatic form which they watch as spectators into a liturgical form in which they participate as worshipers.

This liturgical potential is fully sustained and much augmented in what follows. After a choral opening, part 2 begins with a strongly intensified liturgical emphasis in a procession of priests bearing the banners of the saints Stephen, John the Apostle, and the Holy Innocents, and in a sounding of the Introits of Stephen and John, and of portions of those of the Holy Innocents and St. Thomas. The relationship of Thomas's actions to Christ's through the community of saints and the liturgy is therefore increasingly articulated. At the same time, part 2 is concerned with the community's growing understanding that it is precisely *because* Thomas's coming sacrifice is indeed "for the glory of God" that it can be also "for the salvation of men." In other words, it is through the rendering of glory unto God, and so serving the end for which they were created, that men come to salvation. This purpose is addressed primarily through the Chorus, now become Choir, as the dramatic convention of choral speech in part 1 becomes the liturgical convention of community participation in part 2, a translation essential to the movement of the form from drama through ritual to liturgy, from resistance through surrender to participation.

The part of the Mass that follows the Homily is the Offertory. This involves sanctification of the profane substance, the bread and wine which is to become the body and blood of Christ, but it is simultaneously the preparation of the one who offers the sacrifice, since in the Offertory the celebrant symbolically offers himself to God. In the drama, the scene succeeding the procession of banners has an offertorial significance which is made explicit even before the knights enter and begin preparation of their sacrifice, when the First Priest says of Thomas, "As for the people, so also for himself, he offereth for sins. / He lays down his life for the sheep." Therein he expresses the thematic emphasis of the epistle and gospel for the Feast of St. Thomas, and, as we have seen, of the sermon in the drama. Present throughout this section is imagery of food and drink; as the First Priest invites the knights to dinner, the First Knight sarcastically refers to Thomas in a manner which suggests a profane sacrifice and a debased sacramental meal, "Business before dinner. We will roast your pork / First, and dine upon it after."

After the priests, in something like an offertory procession, bear Thomas to the altar where his own sacrifice is to be made as a type of the Mass-sacrifice, the Action (Canon) or Consecration, commemorating and reenacting the crucifixion upon the altar, is reflected in several ways. As Thomas orders the doors of the cathedral opened to the knights, he cries, "Now is the triumph of the Cross"; and he surely recalls the words of Christ used in the Consecration ("This is the Chalice of My Blood, of the new and everlasting testament . . . which for you and for many shall be shed unto the remission of sins") as, addressing the knights, he acknowledges his own covenant of blood with Christ:

> I am a priest,
> A Christian, saved by the blood of Christ,
> Ready to suffer with my blood.
> This is the sign of the Church always,
> The sign of blood. Blood for blood.
> His blood given to buy my life,
> My blood given to pay for his death.

These and numerous other details sanctify the death of Thomas by identifying it with Christ's sacrifice on Calvary as commemorated in the Action or Canon of the Mass.

The sacrifice in the Consecration has for its purpose the glorification of God; the Communion which follows is a reenactment of the Last Supper, a community participation in the Passion and death of Christ and a figure of community acceptance of responsibility for

Christ's sacrifice, and its special purpose is the salvation of men. So
Communion actions, images, and themes permeate the whole section
within which the murder of Thomas is perpetrated, and continue
through the address of the knights to the congregation. But the community's acknowledgment of responsibility and involvement begins
even before Thomas's death, as the Chorus admits that

> What is woven on the loom of fate
> What is woven in the councils of princes
> Is woven also in our veins,
> Our brains,
> Is woven like a pattern of living worms
> In the guts of the women of Canterbury.

and it continues to their cry, as Thomas is felled, that "we are soiled by
a filth that we cannot clean." In this section of the play, the knights'
tipsiness as they enter to murder Thomas almost appears to parody an
unworthy drinking of the communion wine, in which "he that eateth
and drinketh unworthily, eateth and drinketh damnation to himself,
not discerning the Lord's body" (1 Cor. 11:29). In any case, it is clear
that the knights wish only the slaying (Consecration), and no part of any
meal (Communion) with the priests, so that the sacrifice is in nowise
efficacious for them.

The Communion action is extended to the congregation largely
through the continued use of a convention already exemplified in the
sermon: direct address. Admitting that reasonable people "won't give
us any glory" for the murder of Thomas, the Knights try the faith of
the congregation with the argument that "we have served your interests"; and—ironically—they assume a nonredemptive communion
only of culpability, saying that "if there is any guilt whatever in the
matter, you must share it with us." Whatever the individual response
to the address by the knights and the Chorus, through it the congregation is drawn, forced, to feel some personal involvement, some actual
communion with the events reenacted, so that they both witness and
bear responsibility for Thomas's sacrifice as a type, and even an instance, of Christ's. Thus, the sermon and the so-called apologia of the
knights, as well as other instances of direct address, are not anomalies
violating the form of a play, but uses of a familiar liturgical convention
which, along with the liturgical patterning of the action, *defines* the
form as liturgical. The form is designed, in other words, to affirm the
congregation's theological involvement in the events here reenacted,

and—by stressing his participation in the central event of salvation history—to render each individual inescapably aware both of his share of responsibility for it and of the possibility of his redemption.

In the Thanksgiving after Communion the priest spends some time offering thanks to God for His glory and His mercies. For this purpose the church suggests the use of such prayers as the Gloria. Now, as we saw, no Gloria appeared in the expected place before the sermon, since Thomas then sought not God's glory, but his own; and the Chorus, not yet understanding or accepting God's mercies of blood, was not prepared to celebrate God's glory. But it is entirely in accord with liturgical practice in the Mass and the fundamental purposes of the whole body of the liturgy that here in the concluding section of *Murder in the Cathedral* a redeemed Chorus should on behalf of a redeemed community raise their voices in an exultation indebted to the Gloria in Excelsis, the Te Deum, and the Benedicite in Omnia Opera, praising "Thee, O God, for thy glory displayed in all the creatures of the earth," acknowledging the witness to that glory in the very existence of non-conscious beings and the obligation of men, "Whom Thou hast made to be conscious of Thee, [to] consciously praise Thee, in thought and in word and in deed."

Again, appropriately from the liturgical point of view, the Kyrie, which like the Gloria could not appear in part 1 although it appears in the Mass of the Catechumens, does appear in the last lines of the work. It signals the community's acknowledgment of its need for mediation, its acceptance of Thomas's sacrifice as another yet the same as Christ's, and thus its involvement in His sacrifice. But the Kyrie's appearance here also implies a ritual continuation of the sacrificial action we are witnessing, in a vortical—cyclic, ascending, and accelerating—movement of time and history; a movement in which the swift circle of all creation is ineluctably drawn towards its center in God's will until circumference and center are finally one.

Structural identities and thematic parallels and allusions, then, indicate that Eliot was employing the Mass as a model and control in *Murder in the Cathedral*. But in its deeper nature, the liturgy of which the Mass is the center is said to continue the priesthood of Christ in the present and to communicate the grace of the redemption by ritually reenacting His life; the Mass, that is, may be said to be "a smaller figure" of the life of Christ. Consequently, just as the drama is laden with parallels and allusions to the Mass, so, as William Spanos says, Eliot "shapes the action of Thomas's murder within a matrix of various kinds of verbal and visual references and allusions; which evoke the pattern of the Incarnation: The Coming, The Temptation, The Passion, and The Redemption."

Within this Christological matrix, the Messenger—in earlier editions called a "Herald"—must remind us of the Herald Angels who proclaimed the birth of Christ, and the priests, "watchers of the temple," of those who watched their flocks by night. In this general connection, it has always been recognized that the Chorus's early references to the "coming" and the "Son of Man" as "born again in the litter of scorn" allude to both the advent of Thomas as a type of Christ and the birth of Christ Himself.

Thomas's surprise at facing the Fourth Tempter and his remonstration that "I expected / Three visitors, not four," make it clear that he himself—at this time in arrogant pride—regards this episode as parallel to Christ's temptation in the wilderness (Matt. 4:1–10); and insofar as the first three Tempters represent temptations to gratify the senses, to grasp worldly power, and to abuse spiritual power, they are indeed similar to those which Christ faced.

The sermon introduces Christ's ministry, conceivably with some special reference to the Sermon on the Mount, which immediately followed His temptation in the desert, as this sermon immediately succeeds Thomas's temptation. But, as Thomas says, "Whenever Mass is said, we re-enact the Passion and Death of Our Lord"; and if this statement may be taken to have special reference to Passion Week —the very center of Christ's life, of the Christian year, and indeed of entire salvation history—then it is precisely this climactic portion of the life of Christ which the work most particularly recapitulates, almost day by day.

Accordingly, most readers must recognize the reference to Palm Sunday in the Messenger's description of Thomas's triumphal return from France. The people receive him with "scenes of frenzied enthusiasm, / Lining the road, and throwing down their capes, / Strewing the way with leaves and late flowers of the season," in a fashion both strikingly and ironically reminiscent of Christ's entry into Jerusalem, when "a very great multitude spread their garments in the way; others cut down branches from the trees, and strewed them in the way."

Monday and Tuesday of Passion Week is a time of waiting. Wednesday—Spy Wednesday—is traditionally regarded as the day of the betrayal by Judas, and there is no single or specific counterpart in the play, except perhaps Reginald, the First Knight, whom Thomas describes as "three times traitor" to him and to God. But the key antiphons for the day tell of Peter, who, prior to his fateful denial of Jesus, "sat with the servants and warmed himself by the fire," as he waited outside the house where the chief priest sought false witness against Jesus. The Women of Canterbury unmistakably allude to this incident, and their early wish for noninvolvement in the action of Thomas's coming sacrifice assumes an analogical identity with Peter's wish for noninvolvement in Christ's, when they ask,

> Who has stretched out his hand to the fire and remembered
> the Saints at All Hallows,
> Remembered the martyrs and saints and martyrs who wait?
> And who shall
> Stretch out his hand to the fire, and deny his master? Who
> shall be warm
> By the fire, and deny his master?

Thursday of Passion Week brings us again to the sermon. There distinguishing between the peace of God and the peace of the world, Thomas urges the congregation to "Reflect now, how Our Lord Himself spoke of Peace. He said to His disciples, 'Peace I leave with you, my peace I give unto you.' . . . He said also, 'Not as the world gives, give I unto you.' " The subject of peace did pre-occupy Christ, and He did indeed utter these very words (John 16:16)—at the Last Supper. Once we realize that as Thomas preaches this, his last sermon, in this Mass, he recalls very specifically Christ's words at the Last Supper—the first Mass—we must suppose that his concluding reference to his own impending death is meaningfully analogous to Christ's prophecy of His end, and that Thomas's exhortation to the congregation to "Keep in your hearts these words that I say and think of them at another time" is intended to remind us of Christ's words of commemoration ("This do in remembrance of me" [1 Cor. 11:24]), as He broke bread with His disciples in the Upper Room.

Other events of Thursday are recalled following the sermon. The scenes in the Archbishop's Hall and in the cathedral are Thomas's Gethsemane, and the four knights represent the Roman soldiers who burst in upon the praying Jesus there. Thomas's order to the priests to "Unbar the door" reminds many readers of Christ's command to Peter to put away his sword (John 18:11), and his statement to the knights, "Do with me as you will . . . But none of my people . . . shall you touch," is reminiscent of Christ's words when Judas and the party of captors sent by the chief priests and pharisees came upon Him in the Garden: "Jesus . . . said unto them, Whom seek ye? They answered him Jesus of Nazareth. Jesus saith unto them, I am he . . . if . . . ye seek me, let these [disciples] go their way" (John 18:4–9). And although, like Christ, Thomas is willing to render unto Caesar the things which are Caesar's, the knights' charges against Thomas center about the same point as those of the chief priests against Christ—lordship in the spiritual realm as a threat to secular authority. Additionally, their attempt to get Thomas to admit that he has been traitor to the king recalls by ironic inversion the attempts of the chief priests to provoke Christ to blasphemy before they put Him to death.

Numerous details surrounding the assassination of Thomas evoke the events of Good Friday. Thomas twice refers to his coming death as a "consummation," in what is surely a recollection of the Latin—i.e., liturgical—form of Christ's dying words as recorded in John 19:30: "consummatum est." Thomas explicitly associates his sacrifice with the crucifixion when he cries that "Now is the triumph of the cross, now"; and his last words, "Now, to Almighty God . . . I commend my cause and that of the Church," recall Christ's expiring utterance, "Father, into thy hands I commend my spirit" (Luke 23:46). Incidentally, the choral reference to "heaving of earth at nightfall" calls to mind the scene at Calvary, "when there was darkness over all the land" and "the earth did quake" (Matt. 27:45, 51).

The Mass and the life of Christ, then, are clearly present as related structural and thematic paradigms in *Murder in the Cathedral,* and the remarks of "E" and "A Dialogue on Dramatic Poetry" quoted at the beginning of this essay anticipated at least the first of these. But "E" also refers to the "complete drama," the "full drama of creation" represented in the "ritual of the church during the cycle of the year." And it is evident that this pattern, too, informs the presentation of Thomas's action.

Actually, two cycles of celebration—sanctoral and temporal—operate simultaneously in the liturgy of the church year. The first, to which there is frequent allusion, honors the saints in heaven in whom the work of redemption has been accomplished. Its chief purpose is to keep before the Christian the heroic models of the saints, to encourage him to remain united with them in the body of Christ and the community of saints. But the major cycle is that of the season, the temporal cycle, which repeats perennially for the Christian the principal events in God's scheme of redemption and recapitulates its pattern, in the life of Christ—His advent, Nativity, Manifestation, Suffering, Crucifixion and death, Resurrection and Ascension, and the Descent of the Holy Spirit at Pentecost. The central premise of this cycle is that the Savior of mankind is eucharistically present throughout the liturgical year, living His entire life in His mystical body, the Church; and the chief purpose of the temporal cycle is to give the members of the mystical body the means of living over again with Christ in the present every event of His life here on earth.

This cycle begins with Advent, the preparation for Christ's Coming, and although it originally referred to the historical Coming of Christ in human form, its meaning is extended to His Coming into Jerusalem at the beginning of Passion Week, His Coming into the hearts of believers, and His Coming in glory on the Day of Judgment at the end of time. The season is one of penance and prayerful expectation, and both yearning and fear are moods traditionally associated with it. In the drama, the first suggestion of the liturgical season appears almost immediately, as we learn that "golden October [has] declined into sombre November," that "The New Year waits, breathes, waits, whispers in darkness," and that "destiny waits for the coming."

The Advent liturgy—particularly in the gospels for the second, third, and fourth Sundays—makes much use of the words of John the Baptist, sent from the desert before Christ, as a "messenger . . . which shall prepare thy way. . . . one crying . . . Prepare ye the way of the Lord" (Mark 1:2–3). In the drama, the statement of the Messenger, that "I was sent before in haste / To give you notice of his coming . . . / That you may prepare to meet him," surely reflects the purpose of John the Baptist in the gospel for the third Sunday of Advent, to "Make straight the way of the Lord" (John 1:23). And the response of the Second Priest—"Let us rejoice, I say rejoice, and show a glad face for his welcome"—both expresses the joy which is among the moods of Advent and reflects directly the Introit and gospel for the third Sunday of the season, "Rejoice in the Lord always: and again I say, rejoice. . . . The Lord is at hand" (Phil. 4:4–5). Similarly, the description of Thomas's arrival in terms drawn from the account of Christ's entry into Jerusalem on Palm Sunday directly reflects the gospel for the first Sunday of Advent in the Book of Common Prayer.

That the time of the action passes through the liturgical feast of Christmas is obvious and explicit in the sermon, and there is no need to labor the point; we should recall, however, that the text for the sermon, Luke 2:14, is the gospel for the first Mass at midnight on Christmas Day, and that, as we have said, Thomas's discussion of that text is drawn in terms of Hebrews 5:1–6, which was to become the text of the epistle for the feast of St. Thomas, Bishop and Martyr (December 29).

As part 2 begins, the action occurs in the time "between Christmas and Easter," in general terms the season of the Epiphany, which celebrates the manifestation of Christ's lordship. And while a theme of waiting still persists, the nature of the expectation has changed. As a consequence of the enlightenment proceeding from the sermon, the Chorus now recognizes that "the peace of this world," which they sought at the beginning, "is always uncertain, unless men keep the peace of God. / And war among men defiles this world, but death in the Lord renews it." Recognizing a manifestation of Christ in Thomas, that is, they know what is to come.

Thomas prophesies his resurrection, saying to the knights that "if you kill me, I shall rise from my tomb / To submit my cause before God's throne." As we have seen, all circumstances surrounding the death of Thomas endow it with Easter significance and symbolism, and after his murder both resurrection and ascension are implied by the First Priest, who apostrophizes Thomas as "You, now in Heaven." In the liturgical year, these events are followed by the descent of the Holy Ghost at Pentecost and the institution of the church as the mystical body of Christ. And that pentecostal note is strong in the conclusion of the action, with frequent reference to the church and its renewal by Thomas's death in the Lord; thus it is that the Third Priest rejects despair, seeing that "The Church is stronger for this action, / Triumphant in adversity. . . . fortified / By persecution: supreme, so long as men will die for it."

Since the annual cycle in the church "repeats perennially for the Christian the principal events in God's scheme of redemption, and recapitulates its pattern," the annual cycle of the liturgy is a ritualized projection in "a smaller figure" of the whole history of salvation, past and future—in the present. Insofar as the play is liturgical, then, it must be read as a summary presentation of that history, with the Incarnation at the center separating a period of expectation and preparation before, from a period of fulfillment after. Thus, the Chorus, the "type of the common man," is at the beginning a type of the fallen Adam, of the Children of Israel, in the millennia between Adam and Christ, waiting almost without hope in the darkness of sin for relief from the "various oppression" they suffer. Finally, when they are in the uttermost depths of their despair, God sends His Messenger, John the Baptist, to announce the Coming of the Messiah, who arrives largely unrecognized because born in humble circumstances and who is long unacknowledged because His kingdom is not of this world. After His Coming, history, figured by the rest of the action—while having the profane appearance of an unbroken cycle of sin and death, of fruitless endeavor, and costly triumph ending in ordinary failure—is actually the reiterated acting and suffering required to complete His Passion as a condition precedent to His return from where He sits in glory at the right hand of the Father.

But, since Christ is the end of the Law (Rom. 10:4), with the Incarnation time has been fulfilled, history has already reached its end, and the Kingdom of God is now at hand. Thus the Christian, while remaining in the era of history, through the Eucharist, which proclaims the death of Christ "till he come"(1 Cor. 11:26) at the end of time (1 Cor. 11:11), is introduced even now into the era of the Parousia, the Second Coming.

The point is that ultimately the drama *as liturgical act* presents, as the liturgy itself always does, a vision of the Second Coming at the end of time—*now*. This then explains the mood at the beginning, of fear and dread of "the doom on the house, the doom on the Archbishop, the doom on the world." It explains also both the presence there and the appropriateness of a cluster of lines and allusions with clear eschatological associations and resonances. Thus, the Chorus has an anguished realization that "late late late is the time, late too late"; and the Messenger seems almost to be summoning the Women of Canterbury to judgment as he starkly asserts that "I was sent before in haste / To give you notice of his coming, as much as was possible, / That you may prepare to meet him." This gives special point to the Second Priest's exhortation, "Let us therefore rejoice, / I say rejoice, and show a glad face for his welcome"—certainly intended to recall Paul's message to the Philippians (4:4–5), used in the Introit and Gospel for the first Sunday of Advent, "Rejoice in the Lord always; and again, I say rejoice. . . . The Lord is at hand." But "The moment foreseen may be unexpected / When it arrives. It comes when we are / Engrossed with matters of other urgency"; and although his approach is heralded, Thomas's entrance is sudden and without fanfare; and the Second Priest, preoccupied with trivia, startled and unready, apprehensively begs absolution: "O my Lord, forgive me, I did not see you coming, Engrossed by the chatter of these foolish women. / Forgive us, my Lord, you would have had a better welcome / If we had been sooner prepared for the event." This ambiguous speech must remind us of numerous biblical passages asserting that the return of Christ in glory will be sudden, and at a moment unexpected, passages such as the parable of the Foolish Virgins (Matt. 25:1–3) and Christ's exhortation to "watch, therefore, for ye know neither the day nor the hour wherein the Son of man cometh." And Thomas's laconic statement that "All things prepare the event. Watch," uttered as the First Tempter enters, recalls Christ's parable of the Watchman (Matt. 24:42) and the lesson He drew from it: "Watch therefore; for ye know not what hour your Lord doth come."

This Coming of the glorified Christ is the climax of salvation history and reveals the significance of Christ for all humanity. From this point of view, the central thematic antithesis we have traced between the glory of man and the glory of God—coursing strongly throughout but clearest and most explicit in the sermon—is necessary and inevitable in liturgical drama, as is the movement towards their ultimate identification. But in the Parousia the glory of Christ is extended, not to humanity only, but to all things in the cosmos which are incorporated into His paschal mystery; consequently, the universe, earlier linked with man in sin (cf. Rom. 8:22), is now linked with him in redemption, and is radiantly transfigured into a luminous reflection of Christ's glory:

> We praise Thee, O God, for Thy glory displayed in all the
>> creatures of the earth,
> In the snow, in the rain, in the wind, in the storm; in all of
>> Thy creatures, both the hunters and the hunted.
> For all things exist only as seen by Thee, only as known by
>> Thee, all things exist
> Only in Thy light, and Thy glory is declared even in that
>> which denies Thee; the darkness declares the glory of
>> light.
>
> . . . .
>
> They affirm Thee in living; all things affirm Thee in living;
>> the bird in the air, both the hawk and the finch; the
>> beast on the earth, both the wolf and the lamb; the
>> worm in the soil and the worm in the belly.
> Therefore man, whom Thou hast made to be conscious of
>> Thee, must consciously praise Thee, in thought and
>> in word and in deed.

Beginning, then, as an action with a potential for dramatic development, *Murder in the Cathedral* initially presents an actor profanely playing the part of Christ. But as Thomas perceives that "the true martyr is he . . . who has lost his will in the will of God, and who no longer desires anything for himself, not even the glory of being a martyr," his actions take on the comprehensive and compelling liturgical patterning we have delineated; and this brings Christ to the center in the continuing enactment of a ritual both commemorative and prophetic. The drama is transformed through this patterning of actions and liturgical texts, and through its engagement of the audience as a congregation of worshipers whose heightened consciousness of divine realities merges at the last with the poet's and the actors' as all join in the liturgical act of praise.

In these several ways, *Murder in the Cathedral* gathers past and future into a continuing present which unceasingly proclaims that "Now is the triumph of the Cross, now." The action declares the perpetual contemporaneity of the Passion, until, like the liturgy, it becomes itself a figure in the pattern it displays, and the bearing of witness to the glory of God is finally not so much the subject of a drama as it is more essentially and importantly the exultant purpose of an act of worship.

*M*urder in the Cathedral
and the Saint's Play Tradition

Clifford Davidson

When T. S. Eliot was invited to write a play for the Canterbury Festival in 1935, he chose a topic that had been treated in theatrical presentations at previous Canterbury festivals, where Tennyson's *Becket* had been staged in 1932–33 and Laurence Binyon's *The Young King* in 1934. Eliot's treatment was, however, to be significantly different from the previously produced plays on the Becket story. *Murder in the Cathedral,* to be directed by E. Martin Browne, was designed to touch on contemporary questions of great interest in the mid-1930s, and pay tribute to the greatest Canterbury saint, Thomas Becket, whose martyrdom was to be approached in a way that varied greatly from the usual treatment of the historical drama in the twentieth century. In fact, this drama may be seen as a modern example of a genre that we think of as particularly medieval: the saint's play. Thus it is possible to consider *Murder in the Cathedral* as indicative of Eliot's choice of "medievalism" over "modernisn," and to recognize this as the result of his conversion to Anglo-Catholicism in 1927. Eliot's transformation of a medieval genre, however, involved a relatively complex decision on the playwright's part and also attempted to draw upon some facts of theatrical history which he probably understood imperfectly. He saw his modern saint's play in terms of a connection with ritual and liturgy—a connection which, he believed, would have been present in the medieval genre—and through his interest in ritual forms his drama was greatly enriched.

From *Papers on Language and Literature* 21, no. 2 (Spring 1985). © 1985 by the Board of Trustees of Southern Illinois University.

Eliot may well have known that plays on the subject of St. Thomas Becket existed in the Middle Ages. Interested as the writer was in this medieval saint, it is not impossible that he could have learned from E. K. Chambers's *Mediaeval Stage,* published in 1903 and well known to students of the medieval drama, or from other sources, such as Tancred Borenius's *St. Thomas Becket in Art* or Arthur P. Stanley's *Historical Memorials of Canterbury,* that plays on the subject of Becket were apparently staged at King's Lynn in Norfolk in 1385, where persons were paid for "playing the interlude of St. Thomas the Martyr," and at Canterbury itself, where a "pagent of St. Thomas" was recorded in the sixteenth century on one of his feast days, thought by Chambers to be December 29, until the suppression of his cult. Concerning the Canterbury presentation, Alan Nelson has suggested [in *The Medieval English Stage*] that it was not a true drama, but merely a *tableau vivant,* and not presented for the feast day celebrating Thomas's martyrdom on December 29, but for the eve of his translation, July 2—a much more attractive time of year for an outdoor spectacle. Chambers prints, however, some interesting accounts for 1504–5 and later years, including payments for new gloves for St. Thomas and the painting of his "hede"; armor for the knights and, on one occasion, the necessity of hiring a sword are recorded. The accounts also indicate that a mechanical angel, moved by some kind of device, played a role in the show.

Eliot would have had no way of knowing of further examples of saint's plays of St. Thomas Becket, one recorded at Mildenhall, Suffolk, in 1505, and another at Bungay, Suffolk, at the Chapel of St. Thomas in St. Mary's Churchyard in 1539, a very late date for a play on this subject, since the cult was by then officially suppressed, nor would the modern playwright have known of a play on the subject of Becket at London and recorded in the Skinners' Renter Wardens' Accounts for 1518–19. The London play, unlike Eliot's, apparently presented the entire story of the Archbishop, from his parents' legendary courtship to his murder at Canterbury in 1170. These examples of saint's plays on the subject of Becket were apparently entirely unknown prior to World War II.

There is no question, however, about Eliot's enthusiasm for medieval literature in general and medieval drama in particular. He had studied the medieval theater at Harvard under George Pierce Baker, whose interest in the "pre-Shakespearian" drama included the vernacular plays, most conveniently available to students then in the textbook edited by Alfred Pollard, *English Miracle Plays, Moralities, and Interludes* (1890).

This collection included not only examples of biblical plays from the great medieval cycles, but also an abridged *Everyman,* which Eliot claimed as a direct influence on the style adopted in *Murder in the Cathedral,* as well as selections from the Digby *Mary Magdalene,* one of the two extant saint's plays in Middle English. Professor Baker had also insisted that that his students should know about the early sources of the medieval drama, and advised them to read the liturgical tropes which were the presumed fountainhead of medieval drama.

The so-called liturgical drama, designed to be sung as part of—or as additions to—the liturgy on certain feast days such as Easter or the Feast of St. Nicholas at monastic (most often Benedictine) houses and at cathedrals in the Middle Ages, may be significant for our understanding of *Murder in the Cathedral* because the dramas are ritual forms, and Eliot frequently, even before his conversion, spoke of the close connection which exists—or ought to exist—between ritual and drama. In 1933, Karl Young's monumental *Drama of the Medieval Church* was published by the Clarendon Press. The publication of this book was an event so significant that it is impossible that Eliot, involved as he was in the business of publishing through his association with Faber and Faber, could have failed to know about it. This does not mean, of course, that we can assume Eliot's intimate knowledge of Young's book—indeed, it is likely that he had only a passing knowledge of its contents. Nevertheless, certain aspects of Young's argument seem to agree with Eliot's achievement in *Murder in the Cathedral,* especially his insistence on the close relation of these Latin plays to the liturgy of the Mass and Office. One can only surmise that Eliot would have found the comments on the St. Nicholas plays and their Latin texts most useful as background to his own plan for *Murder in the Cathedral.* As in the liturgical plays, Eliot in his modern saint play insisted on a close association with the liturgy, utilizing in the Canterbury production the antiphons appropriate to the feast day of the martyr and ending the action with the Te Deum, regarded as a traditional conclusion of a liturgical drama and here transferred from Matins to Vespers to preserve this association. Perceptively, Joseph Wood Krutch, reviewing the Federal Theater Project production of *Murder in the Cathedral* in the *Nation* in 1936, comments that the play is reminiscent of "the liturgical drama of the church not the popular if exalted entertainment of the sixteenth-century inn yard." Similarly, Lionel J. Pike has noted that the drama unquestionably "is nearer to medieval liturgical drama than to modern theatre."

Yet David L. Jones can insist that *Murder in the Cathedral* is more closely modelled on Greek tragedy than upon medieval drama, with the exception of "the use of allegorical figures in the temptations scene" and the influence of the versification of *Everyman*. To be sure, the Chorus is adapted from the Greek drama, and additionally the narrative of the play is reduced to its essence, the final period of the saint's life following his return to England and continuing until his death at the hands of his murderers—reminding us more of the condensation of the Greek theater than of the extended story normally told in the medieval saint's play which was based on the saint's legend. Jones's objection, however, must be placed in context, for Eliot saw both medieval drama (especially the liturgical drama) and Greek drama as having evolved directly out of religious rituals. This understanding of the Greek drama owes much to the Cambridge critics whose view of the theater related it directly to its source in the rituals of the cult of Dionysius in ancient Greece. Medieval drama, likewise, was seen as an evolutionary development, a view that was implicitly set forth by Chambers and explicitly by John M. Manly, whose "Literary Forms and the New Theory of the Origin of the Species" was published in *Modern Philology* in 1907. Young's work, likewise, was dependent upon the idea of the evolutionary development of drama out of ritual and utilized the notion that such development must be from simple to complex forms as the organizing principle of his *Drama of the Medieval Church*. As unlikely as Eliot was to have been sympathetic to the idea of the progress of drama from sacred to secular, from simple ritual to complex and humanizing drama, he nevertheless was clearly influenced very deeply by his understanding of the relationship between the forms of worship and the forms of theatrical display. In invoking ritual elements, Eliot therefore felt that in *Murder in the Cathedral* he was returning to elements upon which modern drama had, unwisely, turned its back.

It would thus seem to be crucial to have in mind exactly how Eliot perceived the structure and function of the ritual that, in turn, would so significantly influence *Murder in the Cathedral*. First, it must be understood that he accepted the sacramentalism and ritualism of the Anglo-Catholic theologians of the Church of England which affirmed the role of the Mass in establishing the framework around which life ought to be lived. Richard Hooker, in a passage quoted by Paul Elmer More and F. L. Cross in *Anglicanism* (1935), insists that the sacraments' "chiefest force and virtue . . . consisteth in that they are heavenly ceremonies, which God hath sanctified and ordained to be administered in His Church" and through which grace might be imparted. Also, the rites for the Anglo-Catholic included acts which in some sense not only provide a memory (*anamnesis*) of the past historical events of the Incarnation and Crucifixion, but also somehow bring the events into the present and make the present-day worshippers participants in these events that are made contemporary with them. This view is set forth in the sermon which functions as an interlude in *Murder in the Cathedral:* "whenever Mass is said, we re-enact the Passion and Death of Our Lord." As such, the Mass culminates in the canon in sacrifice, and thus may be called a "Sacrifice." In the rites, God comes into the presence of men, who become actors in the divine drama of suffering, death, and resurrection. So, too, in *Murder in the Cathedral;* the members of the audience are actively brought into the play through the Chorus of Women of Canterbury, with whom they are invited to identify themselves, while the action culminates in a death which ultimately is redemptive within the context of the cult. This action, like the ritual of the Eucharist, is fixed, with specified words and actions repeated each time the play is presented for an audience.

Also, this understanding of Catholic ritual was quite clearly reinforced for Eliot through the intellectual stimulus of early twentieth-century anthropology as applied to the origins of Greek drama. For Jane Harrison, "ritual" was to be defined in terms of the definition of its Greek equivalent, *"dromenon,"* "a thing done." As such, the rite was an act of participation in which the viewers were not merely passive onlookers; in contrast, in drama we have the spectator, for example one who merely looks on as the action is presented before him or her. "It is in this new attitude of the spectator that we touch on the difference between ritual and art," Harrison wrote; "the *dromenon,* the thing actually done by yourself has become a *drama,* a thing also done, but abstracted from your doing." Further, she defines the starting point of ritual in the lack of division between actor and spectator: "It is in the common act, the common or collective emotion, that ritual starts" (*Ancient Art and Ritual*). Thus Eliot in his Chorus uses the women of Canterbury to draw the audience into the "common act," the community of feeling which will respond to the making of the martyr. Rejecting the distinction established between rite and drama by such writers as Harrison, Eliot attempts to mediate between these two categories in his work.

Already in 1923, in the first volume of the *Criterion,* Eliot had insisted that "the stage—not only in its remote origins, but always—is a ritual, and the failure of the contemporary stage to satisfy the craving for ritual is one of the reasons why it is not a living art." The failure of the realism of the "ordinary stage" thus needs to be exchanged for a different mode, "a literal untruth, a thorough-going convention, a ritual." At this point in his development, Eliot's definition of "ritual" seems vague, requiring the kind of examination that he would give this matter during the next decade or so. Eventually he was to take the Catholic liturgy as a standard by which he would view the concept of ritual, which at least after his conversion in 1927 would hardly be visualized merely in terms of "convention" or "literal untruth." Even by 1926, he saw drama as a form that stands in relation to the liturgy, while in 1928 one of the characters in his "Dialogue on Dramatic Poetry" insisted that "Drama springs from religious liturgy, and . . . cannot afford to depart far from religious liturgy. . . . the only dramatic satisfaction that I find now is in a High Mass well performed." Further clarification, however, is provided by Eliot in an article published after the success of *Murder in the Cathedral:* "a religious play, to be good, must not be purely religious. If it is, it is simply doing something that the liturgy does better; and the religious play is not a substitute for liturgical observance and ceremonial, but something different. It is a combination of religious with ordinary dramatic interest." In other words, a play such as *Murder in the Cathedral* may reflect the secular interests of the viewers and comment directly on the world as normally perceived by ordinary people, while at the same time it looks back at a religiously significant event and presents it imaginatively in a way that breaks the normal mould of verisimilitude. But as in ritual, the audience must become a congregation and participate in the act shown on stage.

The role of participation in drama is perhaps to be bracketed with the kind of thinking that Owen Barfield, an author whose work Eliot published in the *Criterion,* later defined as the antithesis of modern scientific and rationalist thought in *Saving the Appearances.* The typical inhabitant of the modern world, characterized by scientific and rationalistic modes of thought that are ultimately destructive, will normally analyze rather than participate, in contrast to medieval man, whose thinking is more likely to be functional, that is, symptomatic of integration into the order of things. Eliot's early poetry was dedicated to the examination of the alienation and fragmentation that characterize existence on the level of the analytic and rational as divorced from feeling. Realism in the theater was, therefore, seen by him as a mechanical contrivance which out of necessity he set out to transcend in his own drama.

As a play on the life of a saint, *Murder in the Cathedral* establishes meaning on several levels at once, though at the same time it appears to eschew excessive reliance on *gnosis,* which would stress the didactic at the expense of the emotional and spiritual planes that are probed in the work. In this respect, it may seem to aim to some degree at a devotional response such as that achieved by medieval saints' plays. Deeply steeped in the sacramentalism which it shares with medieval Christianity, *Murder in the Cathedral* thus dramatizes a classically restricted segment of the hero's life: "I wanted to concentrate on death and martyrdom," Eliot has written. Though the actor Robert Speaight, who originally played the role of Becket, apparently never warmed to the personality of the Archbishop, the action with its tragic and yet untragic death nevertheless was exactly right for the audiences before which it was presented in the 1930s. Becket's temptations and his stoic Christian resolution in the face of death won him the respect of those who came to see the drama first in the Chapter House of Canterbury Cathedral and then in the various theaters in which it played. Thus Eliot could convincingly present a story of a churchman who won the crown of a martyr and who hence could be invoked by members of his cult even unto the present day, his cult having been revived in the Church of England through the efforts of the Anglo-Catholic movement that originated with Newman, Keble, and Pusey at Oxford and, perhaps more importantly, through the Cambridge Camden Society with its interest in architecture and its expression of faith. Canterbury Cathedral, which served as sponsor of the first performance of the play, was itself a shrine dedicated originally to Becket, who also stood in opposition to the officialdom of the state in his day in a way that Anglo-Catholicism had come to appreciate. As we might expect in a drama written by Eliot, its devotionalism is thus far more complicated than that of any actual saint's play from the Middle Ages.

In writing *Murder in the Cathedral,* Eliot had apparently consciously attempted to set aside the kind of treatment that George Bernard Shaw had given to St. Joan and tried instead to establish some continuity with medieval tradition, which he wished to treat with integrity. To be sure, Eliot admitted that he had been influenced by Shaw in his presentation of the arguments of the knights following the murder, but on the whole Eliot's play represents a study of a historical martyrdom in a play which is far more serious than any other English drama on such a topic since the end of the Middle Ages. Thus the hero is a sacrificial victim whose very sacrifice is beneficial to later generations. The dynamics of the martyrdom are identified with considerable clarity by W. H. Auden in an article in the *Listener* of January 4, 1968: "The martyr is a sacrificial victim, but in his case it is he who chooses to be sacrificed. . . . Those for whose sake he sacrifices himself do not choose him as an atoning sacrifice." Hence the martyr is modelling his experience of martyrdom on the Passion and Crucifixion of Christ, who also chose a sacrificial death which his executioners did not appreciate or understand. Eliot's treatment of the martyr's death, we should note, is thus deepened by relating the fate of the Archbishop, the inheritor of the apostolic authority passed on through the power of the keys originally delegated to St. Peter, to the central myths of the Christian religion. The relationship between Christ and the martyr, whether he be St. Stephen the proto-martyr or St. Elphege of Canterbury, or Thomas Becket, is not figural in the technical theological sense, but rather the martyr imitates or repeats the events of the suffering and death of the Savior Christ. So, too, in the medieval play of *Mary Magdalene* in the Bodleian Library Digby MS. 133, the saint at the end not only becomes the model contemplative in her denial of her bodily needs—self-induced suffering, if you will—but also is taken up into heaven first to be fed and then, following the death of her body, to the salvation of her soul. In this play, these effects would have utilized machinery identical with that used for the Ascension of Christ. Thus Becket, for example, will be identified ironically by the Second Tempter as like an "old stag, circled with hounds." The reference here is almost certainly to a verse of the Twenty-second Psalm, "For many dogs are come about me," specified in the Book of Common Prayer as a reading to be read or chanted on Good Friday and understood as a prophecy of the form of the Crucifixion of Christ. Since Becket lives in Christian time, he cannot be a figure or type of Christ, but he can echo in his life the agony experienced by the Son of God who was made to suffer and die as a man, according to medieval theologians. The drunken knights, who appear to kill Becket, are appropriately identified as "Like maddened beasts." Such details as these also have some important implications for our interpretation of the tempters. By extension, these Tempters who come to Becket, internalized and mental as they are, nevertheless do in some sense reflect the temptations that Jesus according to the Gospels had to endure in the desert. The suffering must be preceded by temptations that, to be efficacious, have to be resisted by the martyr prior to his fated end—a fated end that requires acceptance of a higher design.

The pattern of Becket's return and his martyrdom, as well as the subsequent rise of his cult, for Eliot are also analogous to a cosmic pattern that may be observed in nature. As *The Waste Land* illustrates, he was interested in the ritual theories of death and renewal as developed especially in the work of Jessie Weston, whose *From Ritual to Romance* was published in 1920. Eliot would have regarded such theories as indicative of the underpinnings of medieval courtly romance and of folk rituals such as the mummers' plays; additionally, he would likely have included the St. George and the dragon pageants presented in civic pageantry in the late Middle Ages on St. George's Day, April 23, among the items illustrating such themes. Seasonal imagery and the imagery of death and renewal are especially strong in *Murder in the Cathedral.* In the case of one example, the reference to the ploughman's repetition of the turning of the soil in preparation for planting in March, a further level of signification is established, since such a tableau is frequently shown in medieval representations illustrating this month of the year—representations which are part of the traditional series of the Months. In spite of Eliot's now outdated anthropology here, there is nevertheless an element of considerable significance that is added through his references to the cycle of the seasons and to the great pattern of death and renewal, which would see Easter itself as a great festival that parallels patterns established by pre-Christian pagans who in darkness thus prefigured the death and resurrection of the Christian Savior. It is a pattern which includes desecration, pictured in terms of sexual violence and pollution. The sacred place has been made dirty, unclean, as if the very altar has been befouled. In the end, even the air needs to be cleaned in a "world that is wholly foul." That cleansing will be associated with the spring, a season that is as closely identified with hope as the coming of winter is with despair.

The most striking imagery of the play text of *Murder in the Cathedral,* however, is that of the Wheel of Fortune, a ubiquitous medieval emblem that was universally regarded as illustrative of life in the world where ambition and secular *rising* might precipitate a quite different effect from the one desired. Traditionally the figure of Fortuna, blind or blindfolded to represent her indifference to the fate of individual men or women, was placed at the center of the wheel, sometimes turning a crank which then turns the wheel; thus she was presented, though without the crank, as a crowned figure in the frontispiece to the famous Benediktbeuern manuscript which contains the mixture of sacred and profane verse and drama known as the *Carmina Burana*. The modern playwright, who admired Medieval Latin verse, undoubtedly knew the lyrics of the *Carmina Burana* (some of which would be set to music by Carl Orff two years after *Murder in the Cathedral*), though possibly he may not have known the illumination in the Benedickt-beuern manuscript. In any case his drama insists on seeing the wheel almost in Eastern terms as a variant of the Western traditional image—not surprising for one who had studied Indic Philology at Harvard and who for a time had been deeply attracted to Buddhism. Because it is constantly turning, the wheel itself is thus symbolic of the flux of time—the process of temporal transformation—and is hence imposs-ible to control by anyone within time: "Only / The fool, fixed in his folly, may think / He can turn the wheel on which he turns." At the center of the wheel, however, is a still point that is not turning, and from the perspective of this point the turning of the wheel is a pattern apart from the appearance of movement. Understood in this way, the Wheel of Fortune image in the play is absorbed—perhaps through the mediation of an Eastern understanding of the image of the wheel—into another image, which, however, appeared in Western medieval tradition. This wheel seems reasonably identical to the Wheel of Life illustrated in the Robert De Lisle Psalter, which shows God at the center of the wheel. The still point is Eternity, which is beyond time but which provides a point of reference for all time. There is little likelihood that Eliot would have known the De Lisle Psalter's illu-minations, and in any case his choice of this image would more likely have been derived most immediately from Dante (for example, *Paradiso* 3.79–81) and other literary sources. Certainly the image of the wheel is introduced to provide an explanation for the act of martyrdom, which must be beyond this world's flux and the turning of the wheel, if the act is to be efficacious. The lesson is identical to the teaching of the *Commedia,* for example, that the "peace which the world cannot give," of which the Book of Common Prayer speaks, is the peace which can be found only at the center of the wheel. "His will is our peace," as Dante learned in the *Paradiso* (3.85)—a passage echoed in *Ash-Wednesday:* "our peace in His will."

For his sources for the dramatization of the martyrdom of Thomas Becket, Eliot chose to go to historical documents not so different from the ones that might have been available to a medieval playwright preparing a saint's play. Eliot himself denied any extensive research in historical materials. Study of the sources has shown that he was familiar with some of the early accounts of the martyrdom of Becket and not simply with the version that is told in the *Golden Legend.* Hence he is indebted to Herbert of Bosham, who was to have had a speaking role in an early draft of the play, as well as to William Fitzstephen and the monk Edward Grim. From such sources as these he learned that Becket had returned to England in early December, arriving on Tuesday, December 1, 1170. He was welcomed along the way from Sandwich, where he had landed, to Canterbury in a manner reminiscent of the Palm Sunday liturgy and the account of Christ's entry into Jerusalem. He further learned the topic of Becket's Christmas sermon, along with a summary of the saint's concluding remarks in that sermon. So, too, he discovered much about the confrontation with the knights of Henry II which led to Becket's death, as well as about the Archbishop's final words before his end. Since Eliot was concerned to present an authentic representation of the martyrdom, the material in the sources is not misrepresented but handled with the integrity that would be expected of the author of a saint's play in medieval tradition. "I did not want to write a chronicle of twelfth-century politics, nor did I want to tamper unscrupulously with the meagre records as Tennyson did (in unscrupulously introducing Fair Rosamund, and in suggesting that Becket had been crossed in love in early youth)," Eliot explained in his essay "Poetry and Drama."

Access for Eliot to the historical sources would have been easy if he was himself familiar with Borenius's *St. Thomas Becket in Art* (1932), which was reviewed in the October 1933 issue of the *Criterion* by Francis Wormald. Borenius's book thoroughly examines the extant iconography of Becket from the first representation, a mosaic showing the Archbishop at Monreale Cathedral, Sicily, from perhaps no more than a decade after the martyrdom. His first chapter further treats the "life and personality" of Becket and provides, in the notes, references to the biography of Edwin A. Abbott (1898), Latin hymnody in the *Analecta Hymnica,* medieval saints' lives, and the writings of Herbert of Bosham and John of Salisbury, both contained in *Materials for the Study of Thomas Becket* in the Rolls Series, as well as information about the suppression of Thomas's cult by Henry VIII. A quotation on page 8 from the *South English Legendary* likens the progress of the saint from Sandwich to Canterbury to the honor given by the people to Christ as "he rod into Jerusalem"; further, the quotation notes, Becket's death is appropriately compared to the death on the cross of "ore louerd."

Wormald's review in the *Criterion* may well be of the greatest significance for Eliot's understanding of the Becket martyrdom. The distinguished art critic and scholar noted not only Borenius's documentation of the swift dissemination of the cult of Thomas, but also pointed out the three feast days of this saint, which in addition to the feast of his Translation included the *Regressio S. Thomae* found in books for Christ Church Cathedral at Canterbury (December 2) and the feast day of the martyrdom (December 29). These dates in December frame the action of *Murder in the Cathedral,* which dramatizes the return of the Archbishop, his Christmas sermon, and the events of the day of his death. According to the *South English Legendary,* the day of his return to England, December 1, 1170, was the third day of Advent. This penitential season of the Church year—a season when in the English church the Kyrie is substituted for the Gloria in Excelsis in the Eucharistic liturgy and the Alleluia is omitted—was, of course, very much in Eliot's mind throughout the writing of part 1 of the play, which quite appropriately shows the hero of the drama turning away from one temptation after another until, in an ambiguous encounter with a final tempter, he must confront the question of doing the right thing for the wrong reason. Ironically, Advent is the beginning of the Church year, and the warning contained in the Epistle (Romans 13:8) for the first Sunday of the season in the Prayer Book is apt: "The night is far spent, the day is at hand." In the penultimate sentence from the Epistle, the order of all except the last of the temptations in *Murder in the Cathedral* would appear to be established: "Let us walk honestly, as in the day; not in rioting and drunkenness, not in chambering and wantonness, not in strife and envying." The Gospel lesson for this day, from Matthew 21, describes the triumphal Entry into Jerusalem, an event that, as we have seen, was important for both the traditional understanding of Becket's return to Canterbury and Eliot's handling of it in his modern saint's play. Advent is also a period of waiting—waiting in expectation for the celebration of Christ's Incarnation, for Christmas, which also functions as the time of the central segment of *Murder in the Cathedral.*

"The iconography of the martyrdom is fairly simple," Wormald wrote in his review in the *Criterion.* Nevertheless, he notes that depictions of the martyrdom in the arts normally contain three errors. The first, added as early as the twelfth century, was the placement of an altar in the scene, though the murder did not, in fact, take place at Mass but during an evening service. The second and third errors, both logical extensions of the first, show the Archbishop dressed in chasuble and then as a celebrant celebrating Mass. Eliot, though he allows an altar on stage and, as we have seen, uses the structure of the Mass as a device for structuring the play, locates the martyrdom in the cathedral at the time of vespers ("My Lord, to vespers!" the priests urge, and then they literally carry him to the cathedral for the service). In the Canterbury Festival production, however, the preists began singing the Introit for the saint, *"Gaudeamus [omnes in Domino, diem festum celebrantes sub honore Thomae Martyris],"* though no martyrdom has yet occurred. E. Martin Browne thought this liturgical touch was "a brilliant stroke," apparently not recognizing that it was very much like another event told in early versions of the Becket story. This is the narrative account of Becket's requiem Mass; in the *Golden Legend,* the clergy of Canterbury Cathedral were about to chant Requiem eternam "whan the quer began to synge Requiem / An angelle on hye aboue began thoffyce of a martir: *Laetabitur iustus."* Further, the introduction of the Dies Irae "sung in Latin by a choir in the distance," against which the Chorus recites an English paraphrase of the text of this item, seems to make much less specific the liturgical setting for the martydom, while the introduction of the Te Deum, which has been noted above, is an intrusion from Matins. Finally, the play ends with the litany of the saints, which was sung in procession by the Chorus in the Canterbury Festival production, when at the end of the procession there followed the body of Becket, who was carried out through the audience. The conclusion with the litany is a final Anglo-Catholic touch, and we are reminded that even today Mass at an Anglo-Catholic church such as All Saints, Margaret Street, London, is likely to be concluded with a similarly devotional prayer.

In *Ash-Wednesday* Eliot had made much of the internal struggle of the modern Christian between disbelief and despair, on the one hand, and religious belief, on the other. If we keep in mind that St. Thomas Becket possessed the same given name ("Thomas") as the author, we may come to the conclusion that he exemplifies some of the playwright's own agonizings before, during, and after his conversion. Yet such a conclusion is surely false, for Eliot was not writing a personal confession but an impersonal play about an historical figure with whom, paradoxically, he closely identified and sympathized deeply. Like a medieval writer creating a saint's play, he was anxious to present an objective drama—but also a drama which would accurately portray the modern dilemma of both religious and non-religious men and women. Thus, having constraints which differ from those of the medieval writer, he would need to suppress certain devotional elements, though through the Chorus, the Tempters, the sermon, and various other devices he could nevertheless directly make a religious appeal to those sitting at the play, whose participation in the action he clearly regarded as necessary for the success of the production. Unlike Shaw's *Saint Joan,* which is at once entertaining and a didactic experience, *Murder in the Cathedral* illustrates its affinities with the medieval drama of the saints, the miracle plays which were staged primarily as spectacles designed to stimulate the cults of the saints and to provide an impetus toward devotion directed to them. "Blessed Thomas, pray for us," the Chorus pleads at the end of the drama. Thus, too, at the conclusion of the late medieval Cornish saint play of *St. Meriasek,* after the death and burial of the saint, the Earl of Vannes speaks to the audience: "Whoever trust in him / And loyally pray for him / Jesu has granted to them / Their desire readily."

St. Thomas Becket's death in *Murder in the Cathedral* comes after a short speech which reads like the opening passage of a medieval will: "Now to Almighty God, to the Blessed Mary ever Virgin, to the blessed John the Baptist, the holy apostles Peter and Paul, to the blessed martyr Denys, and to all the Saints, I commend my cause and that of the Church." His final statement, however, is only slightly an expansion of his words as recorded in Eliot's source. The result is particularly happy since it is precisely appropriate for a saint's play, for a play which delineates the acts of one who follows in the way of Christ. The Digby *Mary Magdalene* is even more explicit at the heroine's death, for she is made to use language which yet more precisely contains an echo of Christ's dying words: *"In manus tuas, Domine! /. . . Commendo spiritum meum! Redemisti me. / Domine Deus veritatis,"* a passage which is translated as follows: "Into your hands, Lord guide [,] . . . I commend my spirit. You have redeemed me, Lord God of truth."

Murder in the Cathedral is a play which, as Eliot explains in "Poetry and Drama," is designed "to bring poetry into the world in which the audience lives and to which it returns when it leaves the theatre." But the drama is much more than a formal exercise in poetic language; it is designed to bring the saint's play of the past into the present and to make it relevant to the full range of human experience in our time.

Chronology

1888	Thomas Stearns Eliot born September 26, in St. Louis, youngest of seven children of Henry Ware Eliot and Charlotte Stearns Eliot.
1906–10	Undergraduate at Harvard. Discovers the symbolists and Laforgue. An editor of the *Harvard Advocate*, a literary magazine.
1910–12	Studies in Paris at the Sorbonne. Visits Germany. Writes "Preludes," "Prufrock," "Portrait of a Lady," "Rhapsody on a Windy Night," and "La Figlia che Piange."
1911–14	Graduate student in philosophy at Harvard. Begins dissertation on the philosophy of F. H. Bradley.
1914	Study at the University of Marburg, Germany, cut off by war. Residence at Merton College, Oxford. Meets Ezra Pound.
1915–16	"Prufrock" published in *Poetry*, in Chicago, and in *Blast*, in England, 1915. Teaching and reviewing in London. Completes Bradley thesis. Marries Vivien Haigh-Wood, 1915.
1917–19	Employee of Lloyd's Bank. Assistant Editor of *The Egoist*. *Prufrock and Other Observations*, 1917. "Tradition and the Individual Talent," 1919.
1920	*Poems* and *The Sacred Wood*. Begins *The Waste Land*.
1922	Becomes editor of *The Criterion*, a position he holds until its demise in 1939. Dial Award for *The Waste Land*.
1924	"Four Elizabethan Dramatists."
1925	"The Hollow Men" and *Poems, 1909–1925*. Joins Faber & Gwyer, later Faber & Faber, publishers.
1926	Two "Fragments" (of *Sweeney Agonistes*).

1927–31	Becomes a member of the Church of England and a British citizen, 1927. *Ariel Poems*, 1927–31. *For Lancelot Andrewes*, 1928. *Ash-Wednesday*, 1930. *Coriolan*, 1931. *Thoughts after Lambeth*, 1931.
1932–33	First visit to America since 1914. Delivers Charles Eliot Norton Lectures at Harvard (published as *The Use of Poetry and the Use of Criticism*, 1933) and the Page-Barbour Lectures at the University of Virginia (published as *After Strange Gods—A Primer of Modern Heresy*, 1934). *Selected Essays*.
1934	*The Rock, Essays on Elizabethan Drama.*
1935–36	*Murder in the Cathedral. Collected Poems, 1909–1935*, including "Burnt Norton," 1936.
1939	Delivers the Cambridge Lectures (published as *The Idea of a Christian Society*, 1940). *The Family Reunion, Old Possum's Book of Practical Cats*.
1940–44	*Four Quartets*, 1943. Part-time fire-watcher, 1940–41. "What Is a Classic?" 1944.
1946	Lectures in Washington, D.C. Visits Ezra Pound at St. Elizabeth's Hospital. Moves into apartment in London he will share with John Hayward until 1957.
1947	Honorary degree from Harvard. Death of first wife after long illness.
1948	Awarded the Order of Merit and the Nobel Prize in Literature. *Notes Towards a Definition of Culture*.
1950	*The Cocktail Party.*
1951	Suffers a mild heart attack; in poor health thereafter. "Poetry and Drama."
1954–55	Awarded the Hanseatic Goethe Prize, 1954. *The Confidential Clerk*.
1956	Lectures in Minneapolis on "The Frontiers of Criticism."
1957	*On Poetry and Poets*. Marries Valerie Fletcher, his personal secretary.
1959	*The Elder Statesman.*
1961	Delivers lecture at Leeds (published as "To Criticize the Critic").
1962–63	Seriously ill in London. Visits New York with Valerie Eliot, 1963.
1965	Dies in London, January 4.

Contributors

HAROLD BLOOM, Sterling Professor of the Humanities at Yale University, is the author of *The Anxiety of Influence, Poetry and Repression,* and many other volumes of literary criticism. His forthcoming study, *Freud: Transference and Authority,* attempts a full-scale reading of all of Freud's major writings. A MacArthur Prize Fellow, he is general editor of five series of literary criticism published by Chelsea House. During 1987–88, he served as Charles Eliot Norton Professor of Poetry at Harvard.

FRANCIS FERGUSSON is Professor Emeritus of Comparative Literature at Princeton University. He is the author of *The Idea of a Theatre, Dante's Drama of the Mind,* and *The Human Image in Dramatic Literature.*

HELEN GARDNER was Professor of English Literature at Oxford University and an honorary fellow of St. Hilda's College. Her influential books include *Religion and Literature, The Composition of "Four Quartets,"* and *The Limits of Literary Criticism.*

LOUIS L. MARTZ is Sterling Professor Emeritus of English at Yale University. His best known book is *The Poetry of Meditation.*

CAROL H. SMITH is Professor of English at Douglass College of Rutgers University and the author of *T. S. Eliot's Dramatic Theory and Practice.*

KATHARINE WORTH is Professor of Drama and Theatre Studies at Royal Holloway College, London. Her critical studies include *The Irish Drama of Europe from Yeats to Beckett, Oscar Wilde,* and *Revolutions in Modern English Drama.*

MICHAEL GOLDMAN, Professor of English at Princeton University, has written on Shakespeare and on modern drama.

DAVID WARD is the author of *T. S. Eliot: Between Two Worlds.*

Stephen Spender, poet, playwright, novelist, and critic, is also Professor of English Literature at University College, London. His work includes *The Destructive Element: A Study of Modern Writers and Beliefs, Life and the Poet, Eliot,* and *The Struggle of the Modern.*

Michael T. Beehler is Professor of English at the University of Texas, Austin. He is the author of *T. S. Eliot, Wallace Stevens and the Discourses of Difference.*

Robert W. Ayers is Professor of English at Georgetown University and coeditor of *The Complete Prose Works of John Milton.*

Clifford Davidson is Professor of English at Western Michigan University. Among his books are *From Creation to Doom: The York Cycle of Mystery Plays* and *Early Art of Coventry, Stratford-upon-Avon, Warwick, and Lesser Sites in Warwickshire.*

Bibliography

Beckett, C. M. "The Role of the Chorus in *Murder in the Cathedral.*" *Theoria* 53 (1979): 71–76.

Billman, Carol. "History versus Mystery: The Test of Time in *Murder in the Cathedral.*" *Clio* 10 (1980): 47–50.

Browne, E. Martin. "The Dramatic Verse of T. S. Eliot." In *T. S. Eliot: A Symposium,* compiled by Richard March and Tambimuttu, 196–207. Chicago: Henry Regnery Company, 1949.

———. *The Making of T. S. Eliot's Plays.* New York: Cambridge University Press, 1969.

Carpenter, Charles A. "T. S. Eliot as Dramatist: Critical Studies in English 1933–1975." *Bulletin of Bibliography* 33 (1976): 1–12.

Chiari, Joseph. "The Plays." In *T. S. Eliot: Poet and Dramatist,* 115–43. New York: Barnes & Noble, 1972.

Clark, David Ridgley. *Twentieth-Century Interpretations of* Murder in the Cathedral. Englewood Cliffs, N. J.: Prentice Hall, 1971.

Clausen, Christopher. "A Source for Thomas Becket's Temptation in *Murder in the Cathedral.*" *Notes and Queries* 21 (1974): 373–74.

Cuffs, John. "Evidence for Ambivalence of Motives in *Murder in the Cathedral.*" *Comparative Drama* 8 (1974): 199–210.

Donoghue, Denis. *The Third Voice: Modern British and American Verse Drama.* Princeton: Princeton University Press, 1959.

Dukes, Ashley. "T. S. Eliot in the Theatre." In *T. S. Eliot: A Symposium,* compiled by Richard March and Tambimuttu, 111–25. Chicago: Henry Regnery Company, 1949.

Fry, Frances White. "The Centrality of the Sermon in T. S. Eliot's *Murder in the Cathedral.*" *Christianity and Literature* 27, no. 4 (1978): 7–14.

Frye, Northrop. *T. S. Eliot.* London: Oliver & Boyd, 1963.

Ghosh, P. C. "Poetic Drama and *Murder in the Cathedral.*" *Journal of the Department of English, Calcutta University* 18, no. 2 (1982): 90–128.

Goldman, Michael, "Fear in the Way: The Design of Eliot's Drama." In *Eliot and His Time,* edited by A. Walton Litz, 155–80. Princeton: Princeton University Press, 1973.

Grant, Michael, ed. "*Murder in the Cathedral.*" In *T. S. Eliot: The Critical Heritage,* 313–68. London: Routledge & Kegan Paul, 1982.

141

Holloway, Patricia Mosco. "T. S. Eliot's *Murder in the Cathedral.*" *Explicator* 43, no. 2 (1985): 35–36.

Jones, David E. *The Plays of T. S. Eliot*, Toronto: University of Toronto Press, 1960.

Kinneavy, Gerald B. "Becket, the Chorus and the Redemption of Waiting." *Language Quarterly* 22, nos. 3–4 (1984): 25–29.

Kirk, Russell. *Eliot and His Age*. New York: Random House, 1971.

Kojecky, Roger. *T. S. Eliot's Social Criticism*, New York: Farrar, Straus & Giroux, 1972.

Leavell, Linda. "Nietzsche's Theory of Tragedy and the Plays of T. S. Eliot." *Twentieth Century Literature* 31, no. 1 (1985): 111–26.

Lucy, Sean. *T. S. Eliot and the Idea of Tradition*. London: Cohen & West, 1960.

McGill, William J. "Voices in the Cathedral: The Chorus in Eliot's *Murder in the Cathedral.*" *Modern Drama* 23 (1980): 292–96.

Mason, W. H., ed. *Murder in the Cathedral*, by T. S. Eliot. New York: Barnes & Noble, 1963.

Matthiessen, F. O. *The Achievement of T. S. Eliot*, 155–77. New York: Oxford University Press, 1958.

Maxwell, D. E. S. *The Poetry of T. S. Eliot*. London: Routledge & Keagan Paul, 1952.

Osterwalder, Hans. *T. S. Eliot: Between Metaphor and Metonomy: A Study of His Essays and Plays in Terms of Roman Jakobson's Typology*. Bern: Francke, 1978.

Pankow, Edith. "The 'Eternal Design' of *Murder in the Cathedral.*" *Papers on Language and Literature* 9 (1973): 35–47.

Pearce, T. *Literature in Perspective: T. S. Eliot*. London: Evans Brothers, 1967.

Pike, Lionel J. "Liturgy and Time in Counterpoint: A View of T. S. Eliot's *Murder in the Cathedral.*" *Modern Drama* 23 (1980): 277–91.

Pinion, F. B. *A T. S. Eliot Companion*. New York: Macmillan, 1980.

Seed, David. "Eliot's Use of Tennyson in *Murder in the Cathedral.*" *Yeats/Eliot Review* 7, nos. 1–2 (1982): 42–49.

Seyppel, Joachim. *T. S. Eliot*. New York: Ungar, 1972.

Sharoni, Edna G. " 'Peace' and 'Unbar the Door': T. S. Eliot's *Murder in the Cathedral* and Some Stoic Forebears." *Comparative Drama* 6 (1972): 135–53.

Smith, Grover. *T. S. Eliot's Poetry and Plays*. Chicago: University of Chicago Press, 1950.

Spanos, William V. *The Christian Tradition in Modern British Verse Drama*. New Brunswick, N. J.: Rutgers University Press, 1967.

Speaight, Robert. "With Becket in *Murder in the Cathedral.*" *Sewanee Review* 74, no. 1 (1966): 176–87.

Virsis, Rasma. "The Christian Concept in *Murder in the Cathedral.*" *Modern Drama* 14 (1971): 405–7.

Williams, Pieter D. "The Function of the Chorus in T. S. Eliot's *Murder in the Cathedral.*" *American Benedictine Review* 23 (1972): 499–511.

Williams, Raymond. *Drama from Ibsen to Eliot*. London: Chatto & Windus, 1952.

Acknowledgments

"*Murder in the Cathedral:* The Theological Scene" by Francis Fergusson from *The Idea of a Theater: A Study of Ten Plays—The Art of Drama in Changing Perspective* by Francis Fergusson, © 1949, renewed 1977 by Princeton University Press. Reprinted by permission of Princeton University Press.

"The Language of Drama" by Helen Gardner from *The Art of T. S. Eliot* by Helen Gardner, © 1950 by Cresset Press Ltd. Reprinted by permission of Cresset Press Ltd., an imprint of Century Hutchinson Ltd.

"The Saint as Tragic Hero: *Saint Joan* and *Murder in the Cathedral*" (originally entitled "The Saint as Tragic Hero") by Louis L. Martz from *Tragic Themes in Western Literature,* edited by Cleanth Brooks, © 1955 by Louis L. Martz. Reprinted by permission.

"The New Rhythm" (originally entitled "*The Rock* and *Murder in the Cathedral*") by Carol H. Smith from *T. S. Eliot's Dramatic Theory and Practice* by Carol H. Smith, © 1963 by Princeton University Press. Reprinted by permission of Princeton University Press.

"Eliot and the Living Theatre" by Katharine Worth from *Eliot in Perspective: A Symposium*, edited by Graham Martin, © 1970 by Macmillan Press Ltd. Reprinted by permission of Macmillan Press Ltd.

"Fear in the Way: The Design of Eliot's Drama" by Michael Goldman from *Eliot in His Time:* Essays on the Occasion of the Fiftieth Anniversary of the Waste Land, edited by A. Walton Litz, © 1973 by Princeton University Press. Reprinted by permission of Princeton University Press.

"*Murder in the Cathedral:* The Pain of Purgatory" by David Ward from *T. S. Eliot: Between Two Worlds* by David Ward, © 1973 by David Ward. Reprinted by permission of Routledge & Kegan Paul Ltd.

"Poetic Drama" by Stephen Spender from *Penguin Modern Masters: T. S. Eliot*, edited by Frank Kermode, © 1975 by Stephen Spender. Reprinted by permission of Penguin Books Ltd.

"*Murder in the Cathedral:* The Countersacramental Play of Signs" by Michael T. Beehler from *Genre* 10, no. 3 (Fall 1977), © 1977 by the University of Oklahoma. Reprinted by permission.

"*Murder in the Cathedral:* A 'Liturgy Less Divine' " by Robert W. Ayers from *Texas Studies in Literature and Language* 20, no. 4 (Winter 1978), © 1978 by the University of Texas Press. Reprinted by permission of the author and the University of Texas Press.

"*Murder in the Cathedral* and the Saint's Play Tradition" (originally entitled "T. S. Eliot's *Murder in the Cathedral* and the Saint's Play Tradition") by Clifford Davidson from *Papers on Language and Literature* 21, no. 2 (Spring 1985), © 1985 by the Board of Trustees of Southern Illinois University. Reprinted by permission.

Index

145